I-16n

Hunter/Minx

Covers all models October 1966 onwards

Owners Handbook Maintenance Manual

by P Ward

HAYNES   75p

Acknowledgements

Thanks are due to many people for their help and enthusiasm in the production of this handbook.

Further thanks are extended to the manufacturer of the Hunter/Minx range for the use of certain illustrations and to Castrol Limited.

A Handbook in the Haynes Owners Handbook and Maintenance Manual Series.

Edited by Rod Grainger

©   J H Haynes and Company Limited

Published by J H Haynes and Company Limited, Sparkford, Yeovil, Somerset.

Set in 10 point IBM Univers Medium

Printed in England

SBN 0 85696 1450

Contents

Hillman Hunter Super Saloon

Hillman Hunter Deluxe Estate

Introduction

This handbook covers the complete range of cars supplied for the United Kingdom market. It is written for the owner who wishes to find out more about his car and wants to keep it serviced fully, but with the minimum of effort, so that it gives economical, reliable performance.

In this handbook are all the routine maintenance tasks required to keep the car running well, and the tools and other things needed to do this.

All cars over three years old are subject to the official roadworthiness test. Details of what the tester will be looking for, and how to check them yourself, are in this book. Guidance in looking at secondhand cars is given.

Cars are not perfect, and diagnosing faults can be great problem; therefore a methodical guide to fault finding is given. Much time and trouble can be saved if reference is made straight to this book instead of hopping from one thing to another.

If success in tackling the jobs on your car given in this book encourages you to take on more complicated work, a very useful Owners Workshop Manual is available from the publishers, or through all good accessory shops or booksellers.

Hillman Hunter GLS Saloon

Model Identification

The Hillman Hunter was introduced in basic form in October 1966 followed by the Minx in January 1967.

The original 1725 cc 5 main bearing aluminium cylinder head engine is now produced in two further basic forms, the 1500 cc (with a cast iron cylinder head), and a slightly de-rated 1725 cc engine also with a cast iron cylinder head.

The most recent addition to the Hunter range was the introduction of the GLS with a highly tuned engine prepared by Holbay Racing Engines.

A continual programme of minor modifications has been made throughout, but this handbook is intended to cover as comprehensively as possible, information pertaining to all versions.

A wide range of optional extras was provided for most models and included such items as automatic transmission, servo-assisted brakes, overdrive, heated rear window, reclining front seats, metallic paint finish, etc. A wide range of accessories is also available, details of which can be obtained from any Chrysler UK dealer.

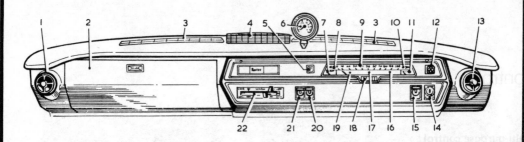

Facia layout: Hillman Minx, GT and early Hunter

1 Directional air diffuser
2 Cubby box
3 Windscreen demisting vents
4 Radio speaker fret
5 Windscreen wiper/washer control
6 Revolution indicator (GT only)
7 Water temperature gauge
8 Left hand direction indicator warning light
9 Speedometer
10 Right hand direction indicator warning light
11 Fuel contents gauge

12 Choke control
13 Directional air diffuser
14 Combined ignition/starter switch
15 Lighting switch
16 Ignition and alternator warning light
17 Headlamp main beam warning light
18 Odometer
19 Oil pressure warning light
20 Panel lamps switch
21 Heater blower switch
22 Heater controls

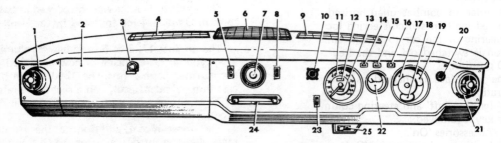

**Facia layout: Hunter Deluxe, Super and GL models
— up to March 1972**

1 Directional air diffuser
2 Cubby box
3 Cubby box lock (if fitted)
4 Windscreen demister vent
5 Panel lamps switch
6 Radio speaker fret
7 Clock (if fitted)
8 Heater blower switch
9 Windscreen demister vent
10 Windscreen wiper/washer control
11 Speedometer
12 Mileage trip
13 Odometer

14 Ignition and generator warning light
15 Headlamp, main beam warning light
16 Direction indicators warning light
17 Ammeter (if fitted)
18 Water temperature gauge
19 Oil pressure warning light or gauge
20 Choke control
21 Firectional air diffuser
22 Fuel contents gauge
23 Lighting switch
24 Heater controls
25 Rear window heater switch (if fitted)

Controls

Multi-purpose control

The multi-purpose control beneath the steering wheel covers the following four functions when the ignition is switched on:-

I   Up and down movement operates the flashing direction indicators and the green repeater lamp on the facia.

II   Movement towards the steering wheel flashes the headlamps.

III   Pressure on the end of the lever operates the horn.

IV   Movement away from the steering wheel selects headlamp main beam and the blue repeater lamp on the facia (dipped beam is with the lever in the central position).

Combined ignition switch/steering column lock (where fitted)

In order to combat unauthorised use, the combined ignition switch/steering lock enables the steering of the car to be locked when the ignition is switched off and the key turned to the O position.

The lock face is marked as follows:- (see illustration).

O   Ignition 'off' and steering column locked when key is removed.

I   Accessories 'On'.

II   Ignition and accessories 'On'.

III   Start position.

(The key can be inserted and removed in position O only).

Unlocking steering column and starting engine

1 Insert key and turn to position 1. The column is now unlocked. It may be necessary to relieve load on the lock by turning steering wheel slightly from side to side before the key will turn.

2 Turn key to position 2 to switch ignition 'on'.

3 To start engine turn key to position 3. Immediately the engine 'fires' release the key and it will then spring back to position 2.

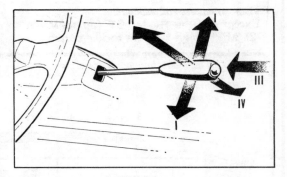

Multi-purpose control *(see text for key)*

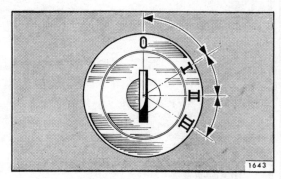

Ignition switch/steering lock *(see text for key)*

To stop engine and lock steering

Turn key fully anti-clockwise to position O and remove. Removing the key from the lock actuates the locking mechanism.

To stop engine without locking steering

Rotate the key anti-clockwise to 1 or 0 depending on whether accessory electrical services are wanted. However, the key must stay in the lock for the steering to remain un-locked.

CAUTION:

Do not attempt to withdraw the key or turn to position 0 whilst the vehicle is in motion.

Windscreen wipers and washers

Except for the Hunter GT (up to March 1972) which has a separate rocker switch, all cars have a combined Wiper/Washer control. The washers are operated by depressing, then releasing, the control and the wipers by turning the control clockwise. The angular position of the control knob also governs the wiper speed on some models.

Interior courtesy lamp

With the lamp bezel rotated fully anti-clock-wise the lamp will illuminate if either front door is opened. The centre position is 'off' and when fully clockwise the lamp is permanently 'on'.

Bonnet lock

The bonnet lock is released either by pulling the remote control beneath the parcel shelf or below the front bumper. The safety catch can then be released.

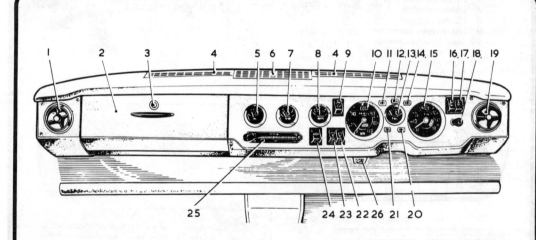

Facia layout: Hunter GT — up to March 1972

1 Directional air diffuser	14 Right hand direction indicator warning light
2 Cubby box	15 Revolution indicator
3 Cubby box push button	16 Main lamps switch
4 Windscreen demisting vents	17 Side and tail lamps switch
5 Oil pressure gauge	18 Choke control
6 Radio speaker fret	19 Directional air diffuser
7 Water temperature gauge	20 Ignition and alternator warning light
8 Ammeter	21 Headlamp main beam warning light
9 Panel lamps switch	22 Windscreen wiper switch
10 Speedometer	23 Windscreen washer switch
11 Left hand direction indicator warning light	24 Heater blower switch
12 Low fuel warning light	25 Heater controls
13 Fuel contents gauge	26 Rear window heater switch (if fitted)

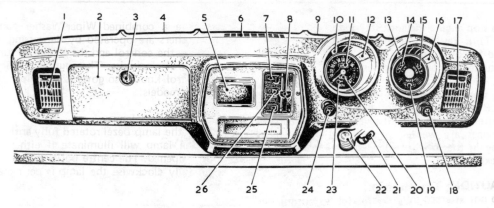

Facia layout: Hunter Deluxe, Super and GL — March 1972 onwards

1 Directional air diffuser
2 Glove box
3 Glove box lock (if fitted)
4 Windscreen demister
5 Ash tray
6 Radio speaker fret
7 Blower switch
8 Heater control
9 Windscreen demister
10 Main beam indicator
11 Trip recorder (if fitted)
12 Turn indicator
13 No charge indicator
14 Fuel gauge
15 Water temperature gauge
16 Oil warning light
17 Directional air diffuser
18 Choke
19 Ammeter (if fitted)
20 Odometer
21 Trip mileage reset control (if fitted)
22 Steering lock/ignition switch
23 Speedometer
24 Windscreen wiper/washer control
25 Lighting switch
26 Panel switch

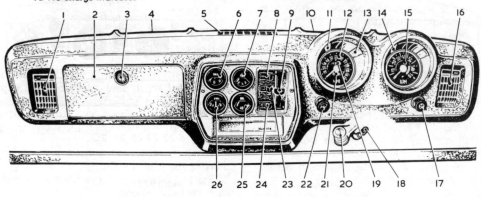

Facia layout: Hunter GLS and GT — March 1972 onwards

1 Directional air diffuser
2 Glove box
3 Glove box lock (if fitted)
4 Windscreen demister vent
5 Radio speaker fret
6 Water temperature gauge
7 Fuel gauge
8 Blower switch
9 Heater controls
10 Windscreen demister vent
11 Main beam indicator
12 Speedometer
13 Turn indicator
14 No charge indicator
15 Engine revolution indicator
16 Directional air diffuser
17 Trip mileage reset control
18 Trip recorder
19 Trip recorder
20 Steering lock/ignition switch
21 Odometer
22 Windscreen wiper/washer control
23 Switch panel light
24 Lighting switch
25 Oil pressure gauge
26 Ammeter

Automatic Transmission and Overdrive

Automatic Transmission

With the Borg-Warner model 35 automatic transmission, driving is considerably simplified. Since the normal clutch pedal and gear lever are eliminated there remain only the accelerator and brake pedals to operate. After starting, gear changing is automatic in accordance with road speed and the driver's requirements.

Two versions of the automatic transmission are available, and in view of some fundamental differences between the two types, it is imperative that the appropriate instructions are carefully followed. In both types, selection is made by a 'T' shaped lever centrally mounted on the floor in a position similar to the normal gear lever for manual transmission.

Early system with L, D, N, R and P selections

The L, D, N, R, P, positions are displayed immediately in front of the 'T' lever.

Operation

To engage L, R, or P the safety button in the end of the "T"-lever handle must first be depressed although the lever can be readily moved between D or N.

The button must also be depressed before the lever can be shifted from P.

L-lock up — This position is used to hold low or intermediate gear which may be advantageous when travelling over rough or wet ground, icy roads or when descending steep hills using the engine as a brake.

D-Drive — This is the position used for all normal driving. Gear changing is automatic according to the position of the accelerator pedal and the demands made by the driver.

N-Neutral — No power is transmitted to the rear wheels in this position.

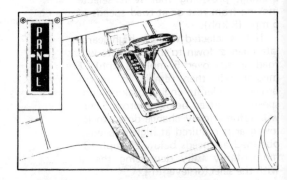

Selector lever - early type

R-Reverse — This is used to reverse the vehicle.

P-Park — In this position the transmission is locked and must only, therefore, be engaged when the car is stationary and the handbrake applied. This position should also be used when making adjustments which involve running the engine.

Starting the engine

Starting is carried out in the normal manner with the brake applied firmly.

The starter switch will operate with the selector lever at either N or P. If the engine stops, the selector lever must be returned to N or P before attempting to start it again.

Selecting L - D - N - R or P

P or R must not be selected whilst the car is in motion. When at rest do not select D, L or R unless the engine is running at idling speed.

Always ensure the brake is on before moving the selector lever if the engine is running.

Excessive "creep" will occur when the brakes are released, if D, L or R are selected above idling speed.

Driver controlled change-down (kickdown)

As long as the car speed is below the maximum attainable in low or intermediate gears, an immediate change down can be obtained by fully depressing the accelerator pedal.

This method of changing down provides more pulling power or acceleration and gives up-changes at higher road speeds.

L-lock up

This position is used to hold the transmission in low gear, for maximum engine braking, providing that it is selected before moving from rest or at road speeds of less than 5 mph (8 kph).

If L is selected when in high gear an immediate change down to intermediate will occur at road speeds over 5 mph (8 kph). The transmission will then remain in intermediate to provide moderate engine braking and when the speed is reduced below approx. 5 mph (8 kph) will automatically change down to low gear. If low gear is required at higher speeds, it may be obtained at speeds below 20 mph (32 kph) by momentarily fully depressing the accelerator with the selector lever in L.

Intermediate can be obtained by selecting L (without resorting to 'kickdown') but this should not be done above 50 mph (80 kph) except in extreme emergency.

Driving on an upgrade

Under prolonged heavy load conditions on an upgrade, L should be selected to engage the indirect gears, thereby increasing the engine cooling fan speed when at reduced road speed. Too high an engine speed in the indirect gears should be avoided wherever possible.

Towing - caravans or trailers

For towing, the automatic transmission fluid cooler and the fluid temperature gauge must be fitted, as it is important that the transmission fluid does not overheat. The temperature gauge covers the range from 70°C to 180°C.
1 Temperatures up to 120°C are quite normal.
2 Provided that the temperature does not exceed 135°C it is safe to drive for short periods. The vehicle should be stopped and checked if the temperature reaches 135°C to determine the cause (eg misuse, lack of fluid etc).
3 NEVER allow the temperature to exceed 140°C as damage to the transmission will result.

Emergency starting

An emergency tow-start may be obtained by initially selecting N, then, when at speed of approximately 25 mph (40 kph) with the ignition 'on' and choke control set, selecting D.

Driving out of mud, sand or snow

If D and R are selected alternatively, with a moderate throttle opening, thus rocking the car backwards and forwards, a good rear wheel grip can be obtained.

Towing - by another vehicle

Unless the transmission is defective the car can be towed with N selected, provided that the fluid level is correct. If the transmission is defective the propeller shaft must be removed and the rear end of the transmission sealed to prevent ingress of dirt or water,

Later systems with 1,2,D,N,R and P selections

The 1,2, D,N,R,P positions are displayed immediately in front of the 'T'-lever.

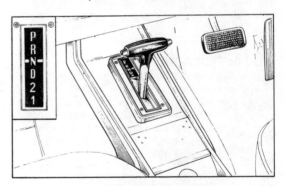

Selector lever - later type

Selector lever movement and positions

To engage 1,2,R or P the safety button in the end of the 'T'-lever handle must first be depressed, although the lever can be readily moved between D and N. The button must also be depressed before the lever can be shifted from P.

1-Lock in low gear

This position is used to hold low gear when moving away from rest (when travelling over rough ground or descending steep hills this may be advantageous). At speeds below 30 mph (48 kph), intermediate gear is selected at position 1 with a further change down to low gear when the speed has fallen sufficiently.

with a further change down to low gear when the speed has fallen sufficiently.

2-Automatic 1-2 or 2-1 changes — If 2 is selected, upward and downward changes between low and intermediate gear only are provided. This may be advantageous when starting from cold or on wet or icy roads. Engine braking is only obtained in intermediate gear.

D-Drive — This position is used for all normal driving. Gear changing is automatic according to the position of the accelerator pedal and the demands made by the driver.

N-Neutral — No power is transmitted to the rear wheels in this position.

P-Park — In this position the transmission is locked and should only therefore be engaged when the car is stationary and the handbrake applied. This position should also be used when carrying out adjustments which involve running the engine.

Starting the engine

Starting is carried out in the normal manner with the brakes applied firmly.

Selecting 1,2, D,N,R,P

P or R must not be selected whilst the car is in motion. Always ensure the brakes are on before moving the selector lever if the engine is running. If 1,2, D or R is selected above idling speed, excessive 'creep' may occur when the brakes are released. The front clutch will also engage with a slight thump.

Driver-controlled change down

At speeds below approximately 35 mph (56 kph) a downshift into intermediate gear can be made by partially depressing the accelerator pedal rapidly. The amount of pedal movement required increases in proportion to road speed until, after approximately 35 mph, the accelerator pedal must be depressed to its maximum amount. This is called 'kickdown'.

Low gear can be obtained at speeds below approxiamtely 25 mph (40 kph) by 'kickdown' action with either D or 2 selected.

Manual control driving

By selection of 1,2 and D in sequence, manual control of gear changing can be achieved. When changing down, 2 should not be selected above 60 mph (96 kph). If 1 is selected, downshift to intermediate occurs and

when the road speed is sufficiently reduced, low gear is engaged.

Driving on an upgrade or over rough roads

Under prolonged heavy load conditions on an upgrade or on rough roads at speeds below 15-20 mph (24.32 kph), 1 or 2 should be selected to increase the engine cooling fan speed. Too high an engine speed should be avoided whenever possible.

Driving out of mud, sand or snow

If D and R are selected alternately, with a moderate throttle opening, thus rocking the car backwards and forwards, a good rear wheel grip can be obtained.

Emergency starting

Emergency tow - or push-starting is not possible with this type of automatic transmission.

Towing - caravans or trailers

For towing, the automatic transmission fluid cooler and the fluid temperature gauge must be fitted, as it is important that the transmission fluid does not overheat. The temperature gauge covers the range from 70°C to 180°C.

1 Temperatures up to 120°C are quite normal.
2 Provided that the temperature does not exceed 135°C, it is safe to drive for short periods. The vehicle should be stopped and checked if the temperature reaches 135°C to determine the cause (eg misuse, lack of fluid, etc).
3 Never allow the temperature to exceed 140°C as damage to the transmission will result.

Towing - by another vehicle

The car can be towed if the transmission is operating satisfactorily provided that the following precautions are taken.
1 Four pints of transmission fluid should be added **above** the normal correct quantity.
2 N must be selected with the ignition 'off'.
3 Maximum towing speed must not exceed 30 mph (48 kph).
4 Maximum distance to be towed must not exceed 25 miles (40 km).

If the transmission is defective the propeller shaft must be removed and the rear end of the transmission sealed to prevent ingress of dirt or water.

Note: The car should not be allowed to coast with N selected and the ignition 'off'.

Overdrive

The overdrive is operated by a switch on the left of the steering column and can only be engaged when either top or third gear is selected.

To engage or disengage the overdrive move the manual switch in the appropriate direction, without releasing the accelerator or using the clutch. The switch should be moved downwards to engage overdrive and upwards to revert to direct drive. (The switch is self cancelling and, therefore, when overdrive or direct is selected, it will return to the central position).

It is usually advisable to select direct drive before changing from third to second gear, thus ensuring the transmission is not subjected to heavy loads due to by-passing normal third gear.

NB: If the overdrive fails to disengage, reverse gear must on no account be used.

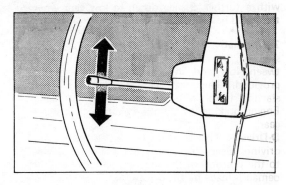

Position of overdrive actuating switch

General Information

Jacking up and changing a wheel
To change a wheel
N.B. If the car is parked on a slope, and one rear wheel is being raised, both front wheels must be chocked.

With the handbrake on, insert the cranked end of the nave plate key behind the nave plate, then twist the key in a horizontal plane. Should wheel trims be fitted, put the key into one of the slots positioned on the perimeter of the wheel trim hub. Steady the nave plate with one hand to stop it springing off during removal. Slacken the four wheel nuts.

Raise the car by inserting the jack spigot in the appropriate square slot provided at front or rear.

Use the wrench to operate the jack. When the wheel is clear of the ground the nuts can be removed.

Replacement should be carried out in the reverse order to removal. Initially tighten the wheel nuts with the car jacked up then finally tighten up after the wheel has been lowered.

Spare wheel
On saloon, the spare wheel is stowed at the front of the luggage compartment and is released by moving the lever away from the wheel (see Fig). When refitting, the knob A may be turned, if necessary, to tension the clamp.

On estate cars, fold back the rear floor covering and remove the rubber plug at the left hand side (see Fig). Unscrew the bolt head using the wheel brace and lower the wheel carrier.

Starting the engine
Do not start or run the engine in a closed garage. Exhaust fumes are dangerous as they contain poisonous carbon monoxide.

Place the gear lever in neutral (automatic transmission selector lever at N or P) and handbrake "ON".

Cold engine: Pull the choke fully out and switch on the ignition, checking that both warning lamps illuminate. The choke can be held in position by turning the control slightly either to the left or right.

Operate the starter. Once the engine has started, progressively move the choke control inwards as the engine warms up to its normal operating temperature. The car should be driven away as soon as possible since the engine will warm up sooner when on the road than it would with the car stationary. Return the choke fully as soon as possible.

When starting the car in cold climates, depress the clutch pedal to reduce transmission oil drag, and release the pedal when the engine starts.

Hot engine: When the engine is warm it will not be necessary to use the choke when starting. Do not agitate the accelerator pedal but if the engine is reluctant to start, depress the accelerator pedal through a quarter of its travel and release it immediately the engine 'fires'.

If the engine is difficult to start when hot, depress the accelerator pedal fully, again releasing it as soon as the engine 'fires'.

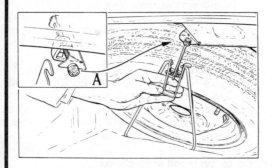

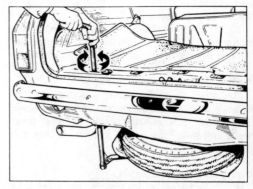

Releasing spare wheel - Saloon
'A' clamp tensioner

Releasing spare wheel - Estate

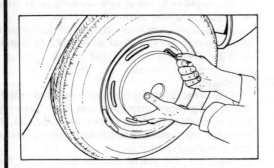

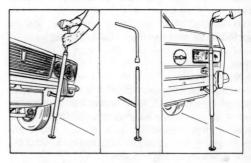

Nave plate removal

Using the screw post jack
Note position of front and rear jacking points

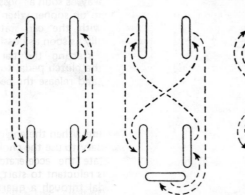

Three different methods of repositioning wheels and tyres to equalise wear

Safety belts
Regular safety checks
It is inportant that the safety belts and anchorage points are inspected at regular intervals for damage and security of mounting.

Cleaning the safety belts
The most suitable cleaning agent for the belts is a mild solution of warm water and soap. Nylon does not absorb water to any great extent and it will dry quickly provided that it is not saturated.

Towing and roof rack loads
If it is required to use the car for towing, it is essential that the correct type of tow-bar is fitted. The total weight to be towed must not exceed 17 cwt (860 kg). If the vehicle is fitted with an automatic gearbox it is important that the special instructions under 'Automatic Transmission' in this handbook are complied with.

If a roof rack is fitted, the total weight carried must never exceed 100 lb (45 kg).

Tyres
New tyres
When new tyres are fitted it is recommended that it is carried out by a reputable tyre factor and that new valve assemblies are fitted. After fitment they should be 'run in' at a moderate road speed for at least 100 miles (160 km) before driving at high speeds.

Tyre wear
In order to achieve maximum service from your tyres, interchanging at intervals of around 5,000 miles 8 000 km) is recommended. Three different methods of interchanging are shown in the Fig.13.

Correctly balanced wheels and tyres are necessary to obtain the best steering and ride qualities, particularly at high speeds. Tyre wear may affect balance, and vice versa. It is advisable to have the wheels and tyres rebalanced periodically, or after interchanging.

Winter tyres and snow chains
Before the use of winter tyres or snow chains is considered, it is recommended that the advice of a reputable tyre factor or approved Chrysler UK agent is sought.

Vehicle identification
Whenever it is required to order spare parts or accessories, the vehicle serial number and service code number should be quoted. Also, when applicable, the engine number and paint or trim code numbers, should also be quoted. Only genuine Chrysler UK parts should be purchased.

The vehicle serial number and paint/trim codes are stamped on a plate which is fixed to the bonnet lock platform. The engine number is stamped on the engine block, immediately above the fuel pump on the right hand side of the engine.

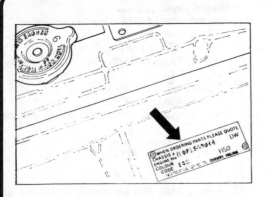

Position of chassis number plate

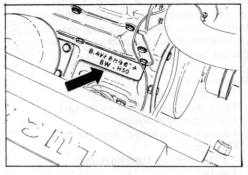

Position of engine number plate

Spares and Touring Pack

Before undertaking any long journey, whether in this country or abroad it is advisable to thoroughly check your car and its contents. It is better to service your car early, before the exact required time if necessary, rather than put if off until your return. Breakdown services, accredited dealers and spare part availability are not always there when you need them particularly abroad and in outlying districts of Great Britain.

There are two lists, one giving spares which should always be carried in the car and the other suggesting those which it is advisable to carry if undertaking a journey abroad. Some dealers are able to supply manufacturers recommended touring packs on an hire/buy-if-you-use basis.

Always carry

First aid box and manual
Spare set of keys (NOT in the car)
List of car main agents
Breakdown triangle (compulsory on the Continent)
Torch (with red flashing dome)
Fan belt
Roll of insulation tape (plastic)
Temporary plastic windscreen
Length of electrical cable (heavy duty lighting)
Spare bulbs for winkers, tail, and brake lights

The tool kit (see next page)
Packet of plastic padding (hard)
Distributor - rotor arm and condenser
Spare spark plugs (2) (N9Y)
1 tin of hand cleaner

Going abroad

The articles in the 'Always carry' list
Tow rope
Top radiator hose
Radiator sealer such as Holts Radweld
Set of fuses
Length of HT lead
Fire extinguisher
Tube of gasket jointing cement
Tin of Castrol Girling Universal Brake and Clutch Fluid
1 quart tin of Castrol GTX
1 spare head gasket set
As many other tools as you feel you may need
Adequate set of maps
List of Chrysler (UK) agents abroad

Always keep this handbook in the car and produce it if you break down abroad. Non-English speaking mechanics will find valuable information about your 'strange' car in it. There are many mechanical terms common to differing languages - you can always point at the pictures; it may help!

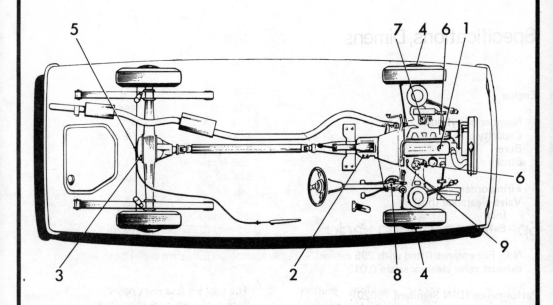

Lubrication Chart

Component	Grade	Castrol Grade
1 Engine	*20W/50 engine oil*	Castrol GTX
2 Gearbox:		
Manual (and Overdrive)	*20W/50 engine oil*	Castrol GTX
Automatic	*Auto-Transmission fluid*	Castrol TQF
3 Rear axle	*Gear oil (SAE 90 EP)*	Castrol Hypoy
4 Hub bearings - front wheel	*Lithium based grease*	Castrol LM
5 Handbrake pull-off springs	*Lithium based grease*	Castrol LM
6 Distributor, starter and		
dynamo bushes	*20W/50 engine oil*	Castrol GTX
7 Carburettor damper		
(Stromberg only)	*20W/50 engine oil*	Castrol GTX
8 Steering box	*Gear oil (SAE 90 EP)*	Castrol Hypoy
Additional items requiring		
lubrication:		
Distributor contact		
breaker cam and		
battery terminals	*Petroleum jelly*	
Hinges, locks, pivots, etc.	*General purpose oil*	Castrol Everyman

Specifications, Dimensions, Capacities

Engine

	1725	1500
Number of cylinders	4	4
Capacity	1724 cc	1496 cc
Bore	81.54 mm (3.21 in)	
Stroke	82.55 mm (3.25 in)	71.6 mm (2.82 in)
Firing order	1 3 4 2	
Valve clearance (hot)		
Inlet	0.30 mm (0.30 mm (0.012 in)	
Exhaust	0.35 mm (0.35 mm (0.014 in)	

N.B. For engines fitted with 295 camshaft (see following performance table) both inlet and exhaust valve clearances are 0.013 in (hot).

Performance (DIN Standard 70020)

	Compression Ratio **	B.H.P. (Imperial) @ rpm	Max. Torque @ rpm
Holbay Engine	9.6 : 1	93 @	106 lb ft
—295 Camshaft	200/210 lb/in^2	5200 rpm	14.7 kg m
	14.0/14.8 kg/cm^2		144 Nm @ 4000
1725 Twin Carb. Aluminium cylinder head			
—298 Camshaft	9.2 : 1	79 @ 5200	91 lb ft 12.6 kg m 124 Nm @ 3800
—295 Camshaft***		79 @ 5100	93 lb ft 12.9 kg m 126 Nm @ 3300
1725 Single Carb. Aluminium cylinder head			
—260 Camshaft	9.2 : 1	67 @ 4800	87 lb ft 12.0 kg m 118 Nm @ 2800
—295 Camshaft***		72 @ 5000	90 lb ft 12.5 kg m 122 Nm @ 3000

1725 Iron cylinder head
—HC 260 Camshaft   8.4 : 1   61   85 lb ft
@ 4700   11.8 kg m
115 Nm @
2600

—LC 260 Camshaft   7.5 : 1   57   84 lb ft
@ 4500   11.6 kg m
114 Nm @
2500

1500 Iron cylinder head
—HC 255 Camshaft   8.4 : 1   54   73 lb ft
@ 4600   10.1 kg m
99 Nm @
2500

—LC255 Camshaft   7.5 : 1   49   68 lb ft
@ 4500   9.4 kg m
92 Nm @
2500

**Compression ratio identification:
   HC = High compression   LC = Low compression (early chassis no. system)
   M = 1500 Low compression   N = 1500 High compression) Service code first letter
   P = 1725 Low compression   Q = 1725 High compression) later chassis no. system

***Commencing serial numbers:
   GL — LH059 7   GL Estate LH150 7   GT — LH031 7

Lubrication system
Pump   Eccentric lobe driven by skew gear on camshaft
Normal pressure   41/45 lb/in^2 (2.9/3.2 kg/cm^2) - engine in new
                                           condition

Filter type   Full flow (disposable)

Fuel system
Pump   Lever operated by eccentric on camshaft
Normal pressure   2¾/4¼ lb/in^2 (0.19/0.29 kg/cm^2)
Air cleaner   AC Delco (single) or Fram (twin) dry element
Carburettor (standard engines)   Stromberg 150 CDS or 150 CD-3 constant
                                 depression type, fitted with manually operated
                               choke (twin on GT versions)

      (Holbay engine)   Twin Weber 40 DCOE with manually operated
                               choke
Fuel octane requirement   97 (89 on low compression engines)

Ignition system
Coil   Lucas 11 C 12 or AC Delco Remy 10039
Spark plugs (all models)   Champion N9Y
      gap   0.025 in (0.635 mm)
Ignition Advance Control   Fully automatic - vacuum and centrifugal
                               (centrifugal only on Holbay versions)
Ignition timing (nominal)   Static 7° - 9° BTDC
                               (1500 LC: 2° - 6° BTDC.,
                               Holbay versions: 6° - 8° BTDC)

Distributor	Lucas 25 D4 driven by skew gear on camshaft (23 D4 on Holbay versions)
Contact breaker gap	0.015 in

Cooling system
Type	Pressurised with centrifugal pump and fan. Sealed system with expansion bottle on certain models
Radiator cap relief valve pressure	9 lb/in^2 (0.63 kg/cm^2)

Clutch
Make and type	Borg and Beck diaphragm spring (hydraulically operated)

Gearbox

Type	Four speed, all synchromesh, and reverse	
Ratios	**Standard Gearbox**	**Close Ratio Gearbox** (GLS and GT from March 1972 on)
Top	1.000 : 1	1.000 : 1
Third	1.392 : 1	1.296 : 1
Second	2.141 : 1	1.993 : 1
First	3.353 : 1	3.122 : 1
Reverse	3.569 : 1	3.323 : 1
Overdrive (where applicable)		0.803 : 1

Rear Axle

Type and final drive: Semi floating, hypoid bevel gears

Final drive ratio	4.22 : 1		3.89 : 1		3.70 : 1	
Overall drive ratio	**Standard Gearbox**	**Close Ratio Gearbox**	**Standard Gearbox**	**Close Ratio Gearbox**	**Standard Gearbox**	**Close Ratio Gearbox**
Overdrive Top	–	3.39	3.12	3.12	–	–
Top	4.22	4.22	3.89	3.89	3.70	3.70
Overdrive Third	–	4.39	4.35	4.05	–	–
Third	5.87	5.47	5.41	5.04	5.15	4.80
Second	9.04	8.42	8.32	7.75	7.92	7.37
First	14.16	13.18	13.04	12.14	12.41	11.55
Reverse	15.07	14.03	13.88	12.92	13.20	12.30
Application:	Hunter d/l Estate (standard 1500 cc)	GT (o/d, March 1972 on)	Hunter d/l & Super sal. (standard) Hunter (o/d) Hillman GT (o/d) GL saloon & Estate (o/d) GT (o/d) Minx	GLS (o/d)	Hunter (standard) Hillman GT (standard) GL sal. & Estate (standard) GT saloon (standard)	GLS (standard) GT (standard March 1972 on)

		d/l Estate (Standard 1725 cc)			

Automatic Transmission

Torque converter — Three element hydrokinetic, with infinitely variable torque multiplication ratio between 1.94 : 1 and 1 : 1 (2.26 : 1 and 1 : 1 subsequent to March 1972)

Gearbox — Hydraulically operated planetary gearbox with three forward speeds and reverse

Overall drive ratios (to be multiplied by torque converter drive ratio)		
- High	3.89 : 1	3.70 : 1
- Intermediate	5.64 : 1	5.36 : 1
- Low	9.31 : 1	8.85 : 1
- Reverse	8.15 : 1	7.75 : 1
	Minx	GL saloon
	Hunter d/l and Super saloon	Hunter
	Hunter d/l Estate	
	GL Estate	

Front suspension

Type — Independent, Macpherson type strut with anti-roll bar

Damper — Armstrong telescopic, integral with strut

Brakes

Make and type — Lockheed hydraulic (self adjusting) front disc, rear drum (Servo assisted on some cars)

Wheels and Tyres

Wheel type — Ventilated pressed steel disc (RoStyle on GT & GL)

Rim size — 4½J X 13 safety ledge; 51 X 13 hump

Tyre sizes	5.60 X 13 Saloons	6.00 X 13	6.00 X 13 Estates	155 X 13 GT	165 X 13 GT	165 X 13 GLS
Rolling radius in. (mm.)	11.4 (290)	11.6 (295)	11.4 (290)	11.04 (280)	11.3 (287)	11.3 (287)
Tyre pressures lb/in^2 (kg/cm^2)						
Up to 4 occupants front	24 (1.7)	25 (1.8)	24 (1.7)	26 (1.8)	24 (1.7)	26 (1.8)
Up to 4 occupants rear	24 (1.7)	25 (1.8)	24 (1.7)	26 (1.8)	24 (1.7)	24 (1.7)
Continuous high speed front	28 (2.0)	30 (2.1)	26 (1.8)	26 (1.8)	24 (1.7)	26 (1.8)
Continuous high speed rear	28 (2.0)	30 (2.1)	36 (2.5)	30 (2.1)	24 (1.7)	26 (1.8)
4 occupants plus luggage front	28 (2.0)	30 (2.1)	26 (1.8)	26 (1.8)	24 (1.7)	26 (1.8)
4 occupants plus luggage rear	28 (2.0)	30 (2.1)	36 (2.5)	30 (2.1)	24 (1.7)	26 (1.8)

Steering

Make and type — Burman F type, recirculating ball

Ratio — 16.4 : 1

Turns, lock-to-lock — 3 1/3

Rear suspension
  Type — Asymmetric semi-elliptic springs
  Dampers — Telescopic direct acting, Girling
    Monitube or Woodhead-Monroe

Electrical Equipment
  Battery type — Lucas D9 (early versions)
    Lucas A9 or F9 (later versions)
    12V (negative terminal earthed)
  Fuses, number and rating — 3   35 amp

  Alternator type — Lucas 10AC (Hunter)
    Lucas 16AC (Hunter from chassis no.
    B 052017039, Hillman GT)
    Lucas 15ACR or 16ACR (Hunter, Hillman GT,
    Hunter d/l saloon from chassis no. LG 063600-
    001, Hunter d/l estate from chassis no.
    LG 085600001, Hunter Super from chassis no.
    LG 074600001, Hunter GL saloon from chassis
    no. LG 058600001, Hunter GL estate from
    chassis no. LG 087600001, Hunter GT from
    chassis no. LG 830600001, Hunter d/l saloon
    from chassis no. LH 064 7, Hunter d/l estate
    from chassis no. LH 160 7, Hunter Super from
    chassis no. LH 075 7, Hunter GL saloon from
    chassis no. LH 059 7, Hunter GL estate from
    chassis no. LH 150 7, Hunter GLS from chassis
    no. LH 040 7, Hunter GT from chassis no.
    LH 031 7

  Alternator control box type — Lucas 4TR (for 10AC alternator) or 8TR (for
    16AC alternator) Not required for 15ACR or
    16ACR alternator
  Dynamo type — Lucas C40 - 1 or C40 - L (Minx)
  Control box type — RB 340, current/voltage regulator
  Starter type — Lucas M35G - 1, M35G, M35J or M35J - PE

Lamp bulbs (all 12V)
  Headlamp (single circular) — Lucas Mk 10 sealed beam unit (60/45 watt)
  Headlamp (rectangular) - with bulb
    (early cars) — 451 (80/60 watt)
    (later cars) — 410 (45/40 watt)
  Headlamp (rectangular) - with sealed beam — Sealed beam unit (75/60 watt)
  Headlamp (twin, 5¾ in. dia.) outer — Unit no. 2A (50/37½ watt)
    inner — Unit no. 1A (50 watt)
  Sidelamp — 989 (5 watt)
  Glovebox lamp (if fitted) — 989 (5 watt)
  Wing repeater flasher (if fitted) — 989 (5 watt)
  Front and rear flashing indicators,
  reversing lamp (if fitted) — 382 (21 watt)
  Stop and tail — 380 (21/5 watt)
  Rear number plate, boot lamp
  (if fitted) — 501 (5 watt capless) or 989 (5 watt)
  Interior roof lamp — 254 (6 watt festoon)

| Panel instrument lamp | 987 | (2.4 watt) |
| Warning lamps, Clock (if fitted) | 501 | (5 watt capless) or 989 (5 watt) |

N.B. Alternator warning lamp bulb for 10AC models is 504   (2.2 watt).
   (A 3 watt is fitted to all other models)

Dimensions	Minx, Hunter	Hunter De-Luxe Super and G L	Hunter G L S and G T
Wheelbase	8ft 2½in (250.2 cm)	8ft 2½in (250.2 cm)	8ft 2½in (250.2 cm)
Track (front)	4ft 4in (132 cm)	4ft 4in (132 cm)	4ft 4½in GLS (133 cm) 4ft 3¾in GT (131 cm)
Track (rear)	4ft 4in (132 cm)	4ft 4in (132 cm)	4ft 4½in GLS (133 cm) 4ft 3¾in GT (131 cm)
Overall length	14ft 0in (426.7 cm) Minx 14ft 1½in (430.5 cm) Hunter 14ft 4in (436.9 cm) Estate	14ft 0in (426.7 cm) 14ft 2¾in (433.7 cm) Estate	14ft 0in (426.7 cm)
Overall height	4ft 8in (142.2 cm)	4ft 8in (142.2 cm)	4ft 8in (142.2 cm)
Overall width	5ft 3½in (161.3 cm)	5ft 3½in (161.3 cm)	5ft 3½in (161.3 cm)
Ground clearance	6¾in (16.8 cm)	6½in (16.5 cm)	6½in (16.5 cm)
Turning circle	33ft 6in (10.2 m)	34ft 0in (10.36 m)	34ft 0in (10.36 m)
Towing capacity (max.)	17 cwt (864 kg)	17 cwt (864 kg)	17 cwt (864 kg)
Roof rack load (max.)	100 lb (45 kg)	100 lb (45 kg)	100 lb (45 kg)

Capacities

Engine sump (including filter)	7½ pints (4.2 litres)
filter	1 pint (0.56 litre)
Gearbox - standard	3½ pints (1.9 litres)
- with overdrive	4½ pints (2.5 litres)
- automatic transmission	11¼ pints (6.4 litres)
Rear Axle	1¾ pints (1 litre)
Steering unit	0.56 pint (0.32 litre)
Coolant (with heater) - Hunter GT	13¾ pints (7.8 litres)
- All other models	12.6 pints (7.2 litres)
Fuel tank	10 gallons (45 litres)

Road Test Data

	Minx 1496 cc	Mk11 1725 cc	GLS
Maximum speed (mph)	83	91	99
Cruising speed (mph)	70	75	80
Cruising range (gallons)	300	270	210
Maximum speed in gears (mph)			
3rd	74	75	77 (non o/d)
2nd	48	49	51
1st	31	31	32
Acceleration through gears (secs)			
0 – 30	4.9	3.9	3.1
0 – 40	7.7	6.3	4.8
0 – 50	12.0	9.6	7.0
0 – 60	17.8	13.6	9.7
Standing ¼ mile	20.9	19.5	17.3
Average fuel consumption (mpg)	30	27	20.5

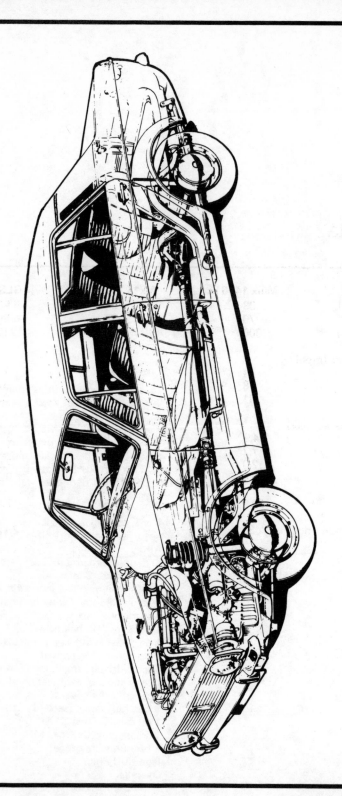

Hillman Hunter Saloon - cutaway

Tools

To carry out the routine maintenance tasks in this book you will need a reasonable set of tools. It would be expensive to buy a comprehensive tool kit at one time. Most people have built up their kits over the years, finding them worthwhile as they tackle more complicated tasks. This spreads the cost. But good tools will last a lifetime. Bad ones fail; they bend or break.

1 set combination spanners (ring one end open jaw the other) sizes 7/16 to 3/4 inch AF
2 double ended box spanners: 7/16 x 1/2 and 9/16 x 5/8 inch, AF
1 set small open jaw spanners: 2 to 6 BA
2 adjustable spanners: one small, one big
1 spark plug box spanner
1 hammer (1lb ball pein)
1 pair pliers with side wire cutter
1 pair pliers, long nosed
3 screwdrivers (small, medium, large)
1 cross-head screwdriver, medium
1 set of feeler gauges
1 file, half-round, second cut
1 oil can (Castrol GTX)
1 grease gun (Castrol LM)
1 tyre pressure gauge
Non-fluffy rag
Overalls
Hand cleanser/barrier cream (Rosalex)

Service Table

Service Interval	Necessary Maintenance Tasks
Daily	Carry out a check on lights, brakes, steering and tyres
250 miles or weekly: (whichever is soonest)	1, 2, 3, 4
1000 miles or monthly: (whichever is soonest)	All 250 mile tasks, plus 5, 6
5000 miles or 6 monthly: (whichever is soonest)	All 250 and 1000 mile tasks, plus 7, 8, 9, 10, 11, 12, 13
10,000 miles or annually: (whichever is soonest)	All 250, 1000 and 5000 mile tasks, plus 14, 15, 16, 17, 18, 19, 20
30,000 miles or 3 yearly: (whichever is soonest)	All previous servicing tasks, plus 21, 22

Each numbered section contains tasks to be undertaken at the appropriate time. These are numbered as sub-sections ie: 1.1, 1.2 etc.

Routine Maintenance

No matter how well you look after your car, various components are inevitably going to wear out and need replacement, but by carrying out the maintenance tasks regularly and punctually the best mileage will be got from them. A great many of the tasks are a visual examination of components; these are vital to the roadworthiness of the car and safety of its occupants. The whole labour of maintenance can be tedious but is essential. Your life or that of an innocent party may depend on it. The care you bestow on your car will be rewarded in freedom from trouble and reducing running costs.

The Routine Maintenance chapter of this book is designed for easy usage. Every task involved in the maintenance of the car is given a number. To use the accompanying table, simply, look down the first column on the left-hand side until the correct mileage interval is found eg, every 5000 miles. On the same line as the mileage interval, set out across the table will be found the numbers of each maintenance task involved at this particular mileage interval. The numbers are set out in numerical order but you can choose the most convenient order in which to do the jobs yourself.

Planning

Before starting work read through what is involved and make sure you have all the parts and lubricants that will be required. As the work will probably be done at weekends or in the evening, garages will be shut. It is most annoying if the job cannot be completed for lack of the stores.

Below are listed the most common things needed. If taken into stock, they will be used in due course, even if this does not happen immediately. In addition to these things there are also the items in the car's spares and touring pack which can be called upon during maintenance.

Garage stock
  Engine oil: 1 gallon (Castrol GTX)
  Oil filter element
  Grease (Castrol LM)
  Gearbox oil
  Brake fluid (Castrol Girling)
  1 set spark plugs (Champion N9Y)
  1 pair contact breaker points
  Antifreeze
  Distilled water (½ pint)
  Vaseline
  Matching touch-up paint
  Rear axle and steering box oil
  Automatic transmission fluid
  Underneath paint
  Aerosol of rust inhibitor/water dispersant such as WD40
  Set of pads for the front brakes

Maintenance Summary

250 miles

EVERY 250 miles travelled or weekly - whichever comes first.

1 STEERING
  Check the tyre pressures.
  Examine tyres for wear or damage.
  Is steering smooth and accurate?

2 BRAKES
  Is there any fall off in braking efficiency?
  Try an emergency stop. Is adjustment necessary?

3 LIGHTS, WIPERS & HORNS
  Do all bulbs work at the front and rear?
  Are the headlamp beams aligned properly?
  Do wipers and horns work?

4 ENGINE

Check the sump oil level and top up if required.

Check the radiator coolant level and top up if required.

Check the battery electrolyte level and top up the level of the plates with distilled water as needed.

1,000 miles

EVERY 1,000 miles, or monthly, whichever comes first - or earlier if indications suggest the safety items in particular are not performing correctly.

5 STEERING

Is there any free play between the steering wheel and the road wheels?

6 BRAKES

Check the fluid reservoir (hydraulic) level. If significantly lower examine the system immediately for signs of leaks.

5,000 miles

EVERY 5,000 miles or six monthly, whichever comes first, or earlier if indications suggest that safety items in particular are not performing correctly.

7 STEERING

Examine all steering linkage rods, joints and bushes for signs of wear or damage.

Check front wheel hub bearings and adjust if necessary.

Check tightness of steering box mounting bolts.

Check the steering box oil level.

8 BRAKES

Examine disc pads and drum shoes to determine the amount of friction material left. Renew if necessary.

Examine all hydraulic pipes, cylinders and unions for signs of chafing, corrosion, dents or any other form of deterioration or leaks. Lubricate the handbrake pull off springs.

9 SUSPENSION

Examine all nuts, bolts and shackles securing the suspension units, front and rear. Tighten if necessary.

Examine the rubber bushes for signs of wear and play.

10 ENGINE

Change oil and filter element.

Check valve clearances and adjust if necessary.

Check distributor contacts gap and lubricate the spindle and cam.

Check fan belt tension.

Check spark plug gaps.

Lubricate the generator rear bearing (not on alternators).

Top up the carburettor damper oil.

Clean the air cleaner element and casing.

Clean the crankcase breather valve and flame trap.

11 CLUTCH

Check and top up if necessary the hydraulic fluid reservoir.

Examine for any signs of leaks if the level has dropped significantly.

12 BODY

See that the water drain holes at the bottom of all doors are clear and that the drain tube from the heater air intake box is clear.

13 AUTOMATIC TRANSMISSION

Check fluid level.

10,000 miles

EVERY 10,000 miles or annually.

14 BODYWORK

Examine the underbody for signs of rust, particularly where the rear suspension is anchored.

Check the condition of the body frame mounting for the upper end of the front suspension units.

15 ENGINE

Fit new distributor contact points.

Fit new spark plugs.

Fit new carburettor air cleaner element.

Flush out the cooling system.

Clean fuel pump sediment bowl and filter gauze.

16 GEARBOX

Check and top up oil level.

17 REAR AXLE
Check the oil level and top up as necessary.

18 STEERING
Remove front wheel hubs, flush out bearings, inspect and repack with grease.

19 BRAKES
Renew servo air filter element (if fitted).

20 HEADLAMPS
Check alignment

30,000 miles

21 GEARBOX
Drain and refill with fresh oil.
Clean overdrive unit filter.

22 REAR AXLE
Drain and refill with fresh oil.

Routine Maintenance

Every 250 miles travelled or weekly - whichever comes first.

1   STEERING
1.1   Check tyre pressures. The correct values are given in the Specifications section.
1.2   Examine all tyres for signs of uneven wear, cuts, bulges or other damage. Remove stones from tread. This is best carried out with the car jacked up, so that the wheels can be rotated.
1.3   Check that the car does not wander when driven in a straight line and that the steering is smooth and accurate.

2   BRAKES
2.1   Test drive the car to check for braking efficiency. Check that during normal braking and an emergency stop, the car comes to rest without pulling to one side.

3   LIGHTS, WIPERS AND HORNS
3.1   Check that all lights, including direction indicators and stop lights, are functioning correctly.
Headlamp beams, particularly for cars with dual headlamps, cannot be readily checked accurately for alignment. Provided that adequate illumination is obtained and other vehicles do not 'flash' their headlamps it is reasonably safe to assume that all is in order.
3.2   Check that the windscreen wipers and washers operate satisfactorily.
3.3   Check that the horn operates satisfactorily.

4   ENGINE
4.1   Check that the oil level is up to the FULL mark on the dipstick. Replenish if necessary.
4.2   With the engine cold check that the radiator coolant level is up to the bottom of the filler neck. Replenish if necessary.
4.3   Check the electrolyte level in the battery and top up with distilled water as necessary. The correct electrolyte level is :-
D type battery - up to the perforated splash guard.
A and F type batteries - with the bottom of the trough just covered.
Other types of battery - just above the tops of the plates.

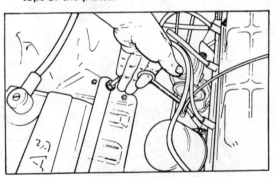

Using dipstick to check engine oil level

Adding oil to restore correct level

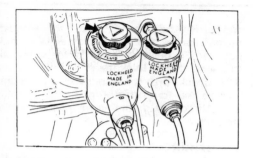

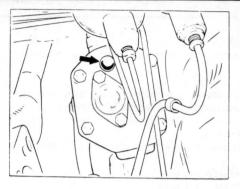

Hydraulic fluid reservoirs/Master cylinders
Brake system arrowed

Steering box filler/level plug

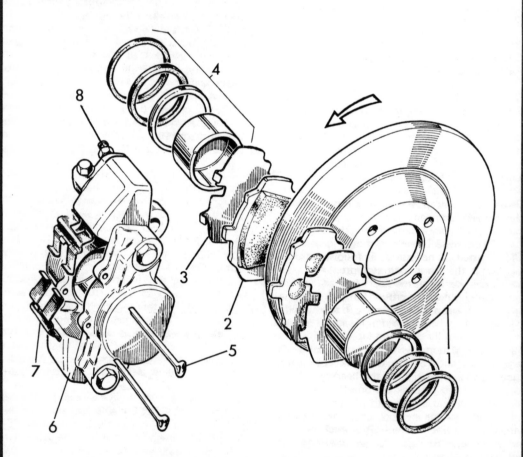

Disc brake assembly *(early type)* **- exploded view**

1	Disc	5	Pad retaining pin
2	Friction pad	6	Caliper body
3	Anti-rattle shim	7	Anti-rattle spring clips
4	Piston and piston seals	8	Bleed nozzle

EVERY 1000 miles travelled or monthly - whichever comes first.

5 STEERING
5.1 Check that there is no more than one inch (approx.) of rotational movement of the steering wheel rim before the road wheels commence to move.

6 BRAKES
6.1 Check the fluid reservoir level and replenish if necessary. If significantly low, examine the system immediately for signs of leaks.

EVERY 5000 miles travelled or six monthly - whichever comes first

7 STEERING
7.1 Examine all steering linkage rods, joints and bushes for signs of wear and damage. This may be facilitated by an assistant turning the steering wheel whilst the inspection is carried out from beneath the car. Rectification is considered to be outside the scope of this handbook and reference should be made to the Owner's Workshop Manual published by J H Haynes and Company Limited or alternatively carried out by an approved Chrysler UK agent.
7.2 Front wheel bearings should be checked and adjusted, if necessary, as follows. Jack up the car at the front then support it on stands under the side frame members so that the front wheels are clear of the ground. Grip the top and bottom of the wheel and rock it to check for play in the wheel bearing. If adjustment is required, carefully prise and tap off the bearing dust cap. Withdraw the split pin from the bearing nut and remove the lock cap. Whilst spinning the wheel tighten the bearing nut to a torque of 20 lb ft, back off one flat then refit the lock cap and a new split pin (alternatively using a tubular spanner tighten as much as you can without using a tommy bar, then continue as described). Replace the dust cover but do not fill with grease.
7.3 Check tightness of steering box mounting bolts. Tighten if necessary.
7.4 Check level of oil in steering box and top up if necessary with Castrol Hypoy (90 EP). The correct level is to the bottom of the filler plug hole. Ensure that the plug is clean and refitted firmly.

8 BRAKES
8.1 Examine disc brake pads for wear.
If the brake pads have worn down to a friction material thickness of 1/8 inch (3 mm) they should be renewed as soon as possible. If one pad is worn on one side of the disc more than the other (this often happens - the inner pad wears faster) it was in order in some early models to change them over; provided, of course, neither has reached the minimum permissible thickness. However, late models and replacement discs are handed. (The pads are identified by a rectangular cut away portion in the trailing edge of the plate). These pads cannot be moved to the other side of the same disc although they can be moved to the same position on the other disc. In order to check pad thickness, jack up the car and remove the wheel. The edge of the pad will then be visible in the caliper which is mounted on the forward side of the disc.

To remove the pads depress the steady springs to relieve the pressure on the split pins and draw out the split pins. If the pads are then rotated upwards a little they can be eased out of the caliper.

When fitting new pads it will be necessary to ease the pistons back into their bores to accommodate the thicker material. First examine the fluid reservoir because when the pistons move back the level will rise and it should not be allowed to overflow. Then move the pistons back by exerting steady pressure with a flat blade between piston head and disc. At the same time check that the anti-squeal cut-out portion of the piston crown is across the line of disc rotation on the lead inside, i.e., upwards in this instance. If it is not rotate the piston carefully until it is. Where the later type pads are fitted, without shims, the cut-out of the piston should be approximately angled at 25° from a line across the direction of disc travel.

When the gap is wide enough for the pads to go in lead in the top edge first and then hold the front lug and rotate the pad downwards so that it fits snugly in position. The shim plates (if used) should be slipped in between the pads and the pistons. (Note that later models and new pads have no shims). Place the steady springs in position with the longer legs facing each other and refit the split pins, spreading the ends a little to keep them in position.

Operate the brake pedal until firm pressure is felt. Then rotate the wheel to ensure

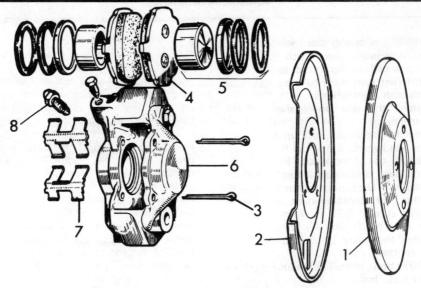

Disc brake assembly (*later type: no shims*) - exploded view

1 Disc
2 Backplate
3 Pad retaining pin
4 Friction front
5 Piston and piston seals
6 Caliper body
7 Anti-rattle spring clip
8 Bleed nipple

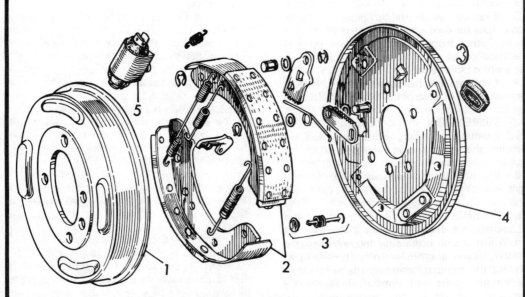

Drum brake assembly (*later type*) - exploded view

1 Drum
2 Friction shoes
3 Shoe steady pin
4 Backplate
5 Wheel (slave) cylinder
6 Shoe 'pull-off' springs

that no binding is taking place (although the pads may noticeably just touch the disc). Always fit new pads of the correct specification and if a different type must be used make sure it applies to both front wheels.

8.2 Examine the rear brake shoes in the following manner:-

Apply the handbrake, jack up the car and remove the roadwheel. Block the front wheels and release the handbrake. Remove the countersunk head drum positioning screw and pull off the drum. Dust out the drum and check the linings for contamination and wear. Provided that at least 1/32 in of lining remains above the rivet heads and the linings are uncontaminated they may be dusted clean and the drum refitted

Rectification of oil contamination or replacement of brake linings is considered beyond the scope of this handbook. Should either of these be required they should be treated as a matter of urgency, but only attempted when reference can be made to the Owner's Workshop Manual. Alternatively the work can be carried out by an approved Chrysler UK agent.

8.3 Examine all hydraulic pipes, cylinders and unions for signs of chafing, corrosion, dents or any other from of deterioration or leaks. Rectification of any of these faults is beyond the scope of this handbook.

8.4 Lubricate the handbrake pull-off springs by application of Castrol LM Grease.

9 SUSPENSION

9.1 Examine all nuts, bolts and shackles securing the front and rear suspension units. Tighten if necessary.

9.2 Visually examine all rubber bushes for signs of wear and play.

10 ENGINE

10.1 Drain the engine oil after a warming up run. Whilst the oil is draining unscrew the filter canister, using a chain wrench if necessary. Replace the element, smearing the rubber seal on the filter base with engine oil. Screw the complete unit on to the engine until just making contact, then tighten a further 2/3 of a turn only. Do not use a wrench. After refilling the system, run the engine then allow to stand for a few minutes before rechecking the oil level.

10.2 Check and adjust the valve clearances, if necessary as follows. The correct (hot) are

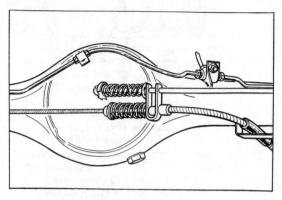

Handbrake pull-off springs

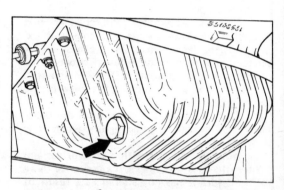

Sump drain plug
(the plug is in the same position on models fitted with a pressed steel sump)

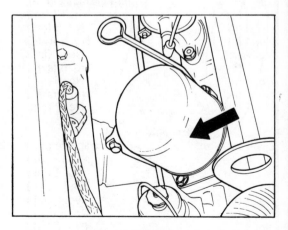

Engine oil filter *(arrowed)*

given in the Specification section of this handbook.

The clearances should be measured and set by using a feeler blade between the rocker arm and the end of each valve stem. This is done when the valve is closed and the tappet is resting on the lowest point of the cam.

To enable each valve to be in the correct position for checking with the minimum amount of the engine turning the procedure and order of checking should follow the sequence given in the following tables. Note that the order is quite different, depending on whichever type of cylinder head (aluminium or cast iron) is fitted. In both the tables below the valves are numbered 1 to 8, starting from the front of the cylinder head. A valve is fully open when the rocker arm has pushed the valve down to its lowest point.

Using a screwdriver and spanner first slacken the locknut on the adjusting stud and then put the feeler blade, of thickness appropriate to the valve being adjusted between the rocker arm and valve stem. Slacken the stud adjuster if the gap is too small to accept the blade.

Turn the adjusting screw until the feeler blade can be felt to drag lightly when it is drawn out of the gap.

Hold the adjuster with a screwdriver and tighten the locknut. Check the gap once more to make sure it has not altered as a result of locking the stud.

Cast Iron Head

Open valve	Adjust clearance (hot)
No. 8 (exh.)	No. 1 (exh.)
No. 6 (inl.)	No. 3 (inl.)
No. 4 (exh.)	No. 5 (exh.)
No. 7 (inl.)	No. 2 (inl.)
No. 1 (exh.)	No. 8 (exh.)
No. 3 (inl.)	No. 6 (inl.)
No. 5 (exh.)	No. 4 (exh.)
No. 2 (inl.)	No. 7 (inl.)

Aluminium Head

Open valve	Adjust clearance (hot)
No. 8 (exh.)	No. 1 (exh.)
No. 5 (inl.)	No. 4 (inl.)
No. 3 (exh.)	No. 6 (inl.)
No. 7 (inl.)	No. 2 (inl.)
No. 1 (exh.)	No. 8 (exh.)
No. 4 (inl.)	(No. 5 (inl.)
No. 6 (exh.)	No. 3 (exh.)
No. 2 (inl.)	No. 7 (inl.)

10.3 Check the distributor contact gap and lubricate the spindle and cam as follows:-

Remove the cap and rotor arm and put one or two drops of engine oil into the centre of the cam recess. Smear the surfaces of the cam itself with petroleum jelly. Do not over lubricate as any excess could get into the contact point surfaces and cause ignition difficulties.

Examine the contact point surfaces. If there is a build up of deposits on one face and a pit in the other it will be impossible to set the gap correctly and they should be refaced or renewed. Set the gap when the contact surfaces are in order.

Examine all leads and terminals for signs of broken or cracked insulation. Also check all terminal connections for slackness or signs of fracturing of some strands of wire. Partly broken wire should be renewed.

The HT leads are particularly important as any insulation faults will cause the high voltage to 'jump' to the nearest earth and this will prevent spark at the plug. Check that no HT leads are loose or in a position where the insulation could wear due to rubbing against part of the engine.
NB If it is required to remove the contacts the procedure in Section 15.1 should be followed.

10.4 Check for belt tension. The belt is correctly tensioned when a total of 5/8 in (16 mm) movement can be obtained on the longest run of the belt. To adjust the tension, slacken the dynamo or alternator mounting bolts then move the dynamo or alternator about its mounting until the correct tension is obtained. Re-tighten all bolts, run the engine for a short while, then switch off and re-check tension.

10.5 Remove the spark plugs and thoroughly clean away all traces of carbon. Examine the porcelain insulation around the central electrode inside the plug and if damaged discard the plug. Reset the gap between the electrodes to 0.025 in. When setting the gap, it is important to note that the outside electrode only should be bent.

10.6 On cars fitted with a dynamo add a few drops of engine oil to the rear commutator bearing. Alternators do not require attention.
10.7 Check the level of oil in the carburettor damper(s) (Stromberg carburettors only). Top

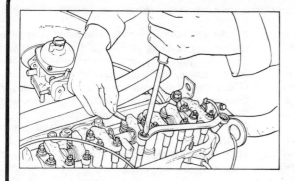

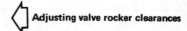

Adjusting valve rocker clearances

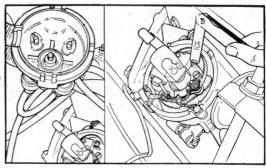

Checking contact breaker gap
Inset - inside of distributor cap showing carbon brush

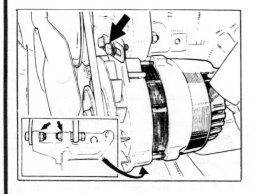

Alternator - arrows indicate bolts to be slackened in order to adjust fan belt tension

Dynamo - arrows indicate bolts to be slackened in order to adjust fan belt tension, and the lubrication point at the rear of the unit

up if necessary to within ¼ in (6 mm) of the end of the bore in which the damper operates, using clean engine oil.

10.8 Remove the outer cover from the air cleaner and remove the filter element(s). This is straightforward on most models but the following instructions should be followed for twin carburettors.

Twin Strombergs: Unhook the throttle return spring on the back of the cleaner, remove the crankcase vent pipe at its flame trap end then remove the four ½ in AF bolts holding the air cleaner to the two carburettor flanges. Lift off the air cleaner as a complete assembly taking care not to lose the two joints used between the air cleaner and carburettor.

Twin Weber (GLS model): Initially turn the front wheels on to right lock then release the clip holding the air intake flexible pipe to the carburettor air box. Draw off the pipe. Remove the two 7/16 in AF screws and one ½ in AF nut that secure the cleaner to the wing valance and lift away cleaner. Do not lose washers under ½ in AF nut. Unscrew wing nut on air cleaner and remove cover.

In all cases wipe or blow out dust from filter casing. Dust on the outside of filter elements can be removed with low pressure compressed air, used carefully at an angle so that it does not blow into the element.

Do not use any liquid solvents or oil the element in any way.

Reassemble in the reverse order to dismantling.

10.9 To clean the crankcase breather flame trap detach the rubber connecting hoses then soak the trap in a paraffin bath. Swill to loosen dirt particles then allow to drain. Finally dry with a low pressure air line. Do not clean in petrol.

11   CLUTCH
11.1 Check the fluid level in the clutch reservoir. Top up if necessary. Examine system for leaks if the level has dropped significantly.

12   BODY
12.1 Check that the water drain holes at the bottom of all doors are clean and that the drain tube from the heater air intake is clear.

13   AUTOMATIC TRANSMISSION
13.1 Automatic transmission fluid level should be checked as follows:- Run the car for about 5 miles (8 km) then select P and allow the engine

to idle for approximately 2 minutes. With the engine still running remove and wipe clean the dipstick. Refit and check fluid level with the engine still running at idling speed. Top up to HIGH level if necessary, but do not overfill. If frequent topping up is required, the advice of a Chrysler UK agent should be sought.

13.2 Check that the slots, grilles and transmission fluid pan are free from all contamination such as underseal, mud, etc.

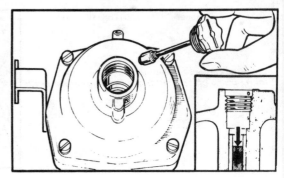

Stromberg carburettor - dashpot damper removed
Inset - correct oil level in damper bore

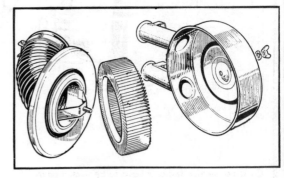

Air cleaner (GLS) - exploded view

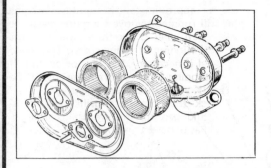

Air cleaner *(GT)* - exploded view

Air cleaner *(Deluxe)* - exploded view

Flame trap *(arrowed)*

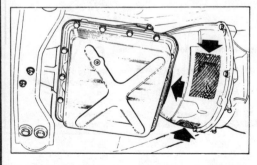

Underside of automatic transmission unit showing cooling ducts *(arrowed)*

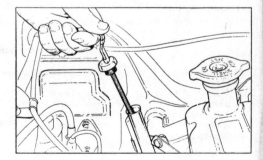

Checking fluid level of automatic transmission unit

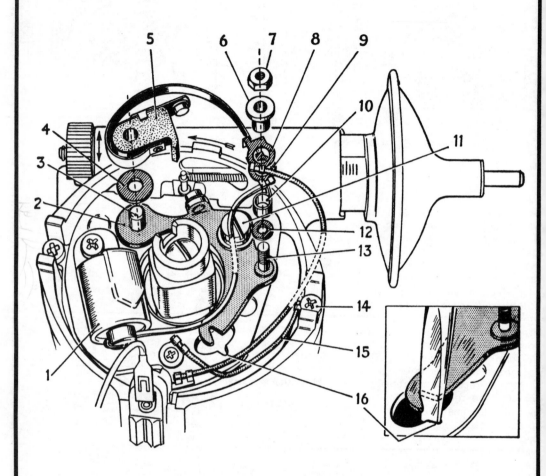

Contact breaker points - exploded view

1 Condenser
2 Fixed contact plate
3 Moving contact pivot post
4 Fibre insulating washer
5 Moving contact
6 Nylon insulating sleeve
7 Terminal nut
8 Lead from coil
9 Lead to condenser
10 Moving contact spring eye
11 Fixed contact plate securing screw
12 Fibre insulating washer
13 Terminal post
14 Contact base plate
securing screw (and earth wire connection)
15 Earth wire
16 Screwdriver notch for adjustment

EVERY 10,000 miles travelled or annually - whichever comes first

14   BODYWORK

14.1 Examine the underbody for signs of rust, particularly where the rear suspension is anchored. Check also the condition of the body frame mounting for the upper end of the front suspension units. If rust or deterioration is noted it is recommended that the advice of a Chrysler UK agent is sought for remedial action.

15   ENGINE

15.1 Fit new distributor contact points as follows.

Remove the distributor cap and rotor arm and remove the fixed plate locking screw. Undo the small nut on the terminal post which also secures the end of the spring and lift off the washer and nylon insulating sleeve. The two circular tags from the coil and condenser leads may then be taken off and the spring contact lifted off at the pivot post. The fixed contact can also now be lifted out.

Replacement is a reversal of the removal procedure. Modern contact sets are sometimes supplied as a complete assembly which can be fitted and connected as a single unit. If the new points are in separate pieces the assembly on the terminal post is very important. If you did not notice the order in which the pieces came off, the correct order of replacement is - Fixed contact onto the base plate, insulating washer over the terminal post (NOT the pivot post), spring contact, lead connectors onto terminal post, nylon sleeve on terminal post, plain washer and nut. This assembly insulates the spring side of the contacts from earth except when the points are closed. Reset contact gap on completion.

15.2 Fit new spark plugs of the recommended type with correctly set gaps.

15.3 Renew the carburettor air cleaner element(s). See Section 10.8 for removal procedure.

15.4 Flush out the cooling system using a proprietary cleaning agent which does not contain caustic soda. Initially set the heater control to HOT then open the drain plugs on the radiator and cylinder block. Follow the manufacturer's instructions for the particular cleaning agent used.

15.5 To clean the fuel pump filter unscrew the nut on top of the cover and spring the clip to

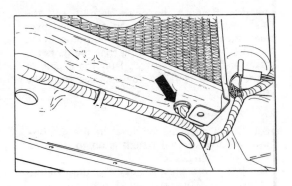

Radiator drain tap *(arrowed)*

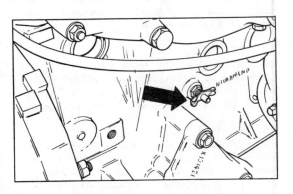

Cylinder block drain tap *(arrowed)*

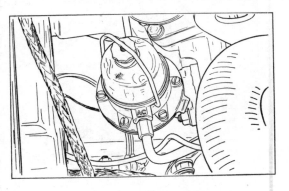

Fuel pump

one side. Remove the cover and lift out the filter. Wash the filter in clean petrol and then clean the sediment chamber in the pump. Refit the filter and cover, ensuring that the gasket is intact and properly seated. Run the engine to check that there is no fuel leakage from the cover.

16   GEARBOX
16.1 Check that the oil level in the gearbox (and overdrive unit if fitted) is up to the level of the filler plug.
NB Clean the area around the plug before commencing. Top up level if necessary, with appropriate oil.

17   REAR AXLE
17.1 Check rear axle oil level using the same procedure as for the gearbox. Top up if necessary, with the appropriate oil.

18   STEERING
18.1 Removal of the front wheel hubs and re-greasing the bearing is considered beyond the scope of this handbook. Consult the Owners Workshop Manual or your Chrysler UK agent.

19   BRAKES
19.1 Lift off the filter cover from the servo unit (where fitted) then remove the spring, filter and sorbo washer. Position the washer, new filter and spring then place the cover on the washer and press downwards so that it snaps, into position.

20   HEADLAMPS
20.1 Arrange for the headlamp alignment to be checked by an approved Chrysler UK agent.

EVERY 30,000 miles or 3 years - whichever comes first
21   GEARBOX
21.1 Prior to draining the oil from the gearbox, the car should be run for sufficient time to allow the gear oil to thin down a little. Remove filler and drain plugs for gearbox and drain plug from overdrive (where fitted). Allow to drain for 15 minutes then replace drain plug(s) preferably with new washers and refill to the filler level hole, with the appropriate oil. Replace plug on completion.

21.2 To remove the filter from the overdrive for cleaning, unscrew the four retaining bolts then take off the cover plate and gasket. Clean the filter in paraffin and dry thoroughly before re-assembling. Ensure the three magnetic rings are fitted into the filter, followed by the large diameter sealing ring. This is to be fitted with its rubber face towards the filter.

22   REAR AXLE
22.1 Remove the level/filler plug and drain plug, after a warming up run, and drain out the oil. After about 10 minutes refit the drain plug and refill to the level of the filler hole, with appropriate oil. Replace the level/filler plug.

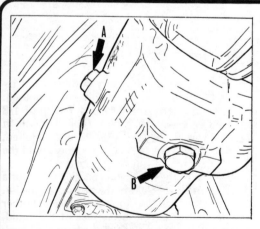

Gearbox lubrication
filler plug A; drain plug B

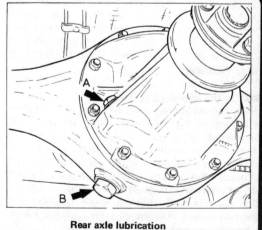

Rear axle lubrication
filler plug A; drain plug B

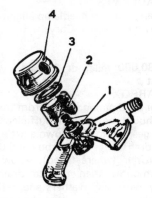

Servo unit air filter assembly - exploded view

1 *Air valve and air valve return spring*
2 *Air filter*
3 *Sorbo washer*
4 *Air valve cover dome*

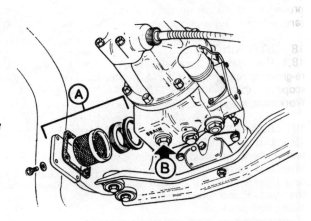

Overdrive unit maintenance

Exploded view of filter assembly A; drain plug B

ther Maintenance

eeding the hydraulic system

The system should need bleeding only when
me part of the system has been dismantled
ich would allow air into the fluid circuit; or
the reservoir level has been allowed to drop
far that air has entered the master cylinder.
Ensure that a supply of clean non-aerated
id of the correct specification is to hand in
der to replenish the reservoir during the
eeding process. It is advisable, if not essential,
 have someone available to help, as one
rson has to pump the brake pedal while the
her attends to each wheel. The reservoir level

has also to be continuously watched and re-
plenished. Fluid bled out should not be re-used.
A clean glass jar and a 9-12 inch length of 1/8
inch internal diamter rubber tube that will fit
tightly over the bleed nipples is also required.

Bleed the front brakes first as these hold the
largest quantity of fluid in the system.

Make sure the bleed nipple is clean and put a
small quantity of fluid in the bottom of the jar.
Fit the tube onto the nipple and place the other
end in the jar under the surface of the liquid.
Keep it under the surface throughout the bleeding operation.

Unscrew the bleed screw ½ turn and get the
assistant to depress and release the brake pedal

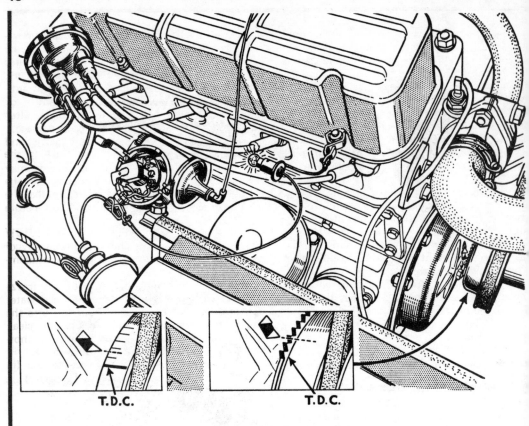

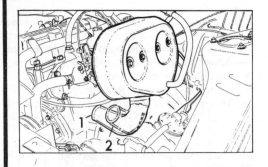

T.D.C.   T.D.C.

Static ignition timing diagram
Insets show alternative timing marks both reading 8º BTDC

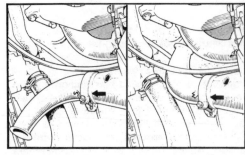

Air cleaner intake *(GT)* **showing alternative positions**
Winter 1; Summer 2

Air cleaner intake *(Deluxe)* **showing Summer and Winter positions**

in short sharp bursts when you direct him. Short sharp jabs are better than long slow ones because they will force any air bubbles along the line ahead of the fluid rather than pump the fluid past them. It is not essential to remove all the air the first time. If the whole system is being bled, attend to each wheel for three or four complete pedal strokes and then repeat the process. On the second time around operate the pedal sharply in the same way until no more bubbles are apparent. The bleed screw should be tightened and closed with the brake pedal fully depressed which ensures that no aerated fluid can get back into the system. Do not forget to keep the reservoir topped up throughout.

When all four wheels have been satisfactorily bled depress the foot pedal which should offer a firm resistance with no trace of 'sponginess'. The pedal should not continue to go down under sustained pressure. If it does there is a leak or the master cylinder seals are worn out.

Ignition timing

To check the ignition timing, set the contact gap to 0.015 in, then connect a 12v bulb between the LT distributor lead and a good earth. Using a 15/16 in AF spanner turn the crankshaft clockwise until the bulb just lights indicating the contacts are open. Check, using the timing marks on the pulley and timing case, that the timing is in accordance with that given in the General Data section of this handbook. Note - the marks on the pulley are at 5° intervals.

Winter motoring

Anti-freeze

Anti-freeze liquid added to the coolant is now the accepted protection against cold which can freeze the coolant and crack the block. Even though a heater may be available whilst the car is garaged at night, daytime temperatures when the car is parked outside can be low enough to freeze! At very low temperatures the coolant in the lower half of the radiator can freeze when the engine is running, if anti-freeze is not used. Also a small quantity of water will always remain in the block after draining which could freeze and cause damage.

Anti-freeze has very searching properties and if there are any leaks or near leaks in the system, it will accentuate them and you may soon notice growths of bluish deposits at the offending places. Make sure, therefore, that the cooling system is in good condition before adding anti-freeze.

Use only anti-freeze liquid to B.S. 3151/ 3152 which will be an inhibited ethylene glycol mixture. Inhibited to protect attacks on aluminium alloy components.

Mix the required quantity of anti-freeze liquid with half the quantity of clean water required to fill the system. Pour this into the flushed out radiator and top up with clean water. Run the engine straight away to thoroughly disperse the anti-freeze throughout.

The percentages of anti-freeze to use (in relation to the total cooling liquid capacity) are given in the table below:-

Solution strength	Frost protection	Safe pump circulation
25%	-15^oF (-26^oC)	10^oF (-12^oC)
30%	-28^oF (-33^oC)	3^oF (-16^oC)
35%	-38^oF (-39^oC)	-4^oF (-20^oC)
40%	-42^oF (-41^oC)	-10^oF (-23^oC)
50%	-53^oF (-47^oC)	-32^oF (-36^oC)

Carburettors

On carburettors with movable air cleaner inlets, the inlet pipe should be moved towards the engine exhaust manifold for winter driving, to supply the carburettor with warm air.

Bodywork - maintenance, cleaning, minor repairs

Car cleaning - interior

First empty the car completely - from shelves and trays to under the seats - of all the paraphernalia of travel.

Lift out the rubber mats, carpeting and underfelt. The rubber mats should be washed. The carpets may be brushed, shaken or beaten to remove the dust and dirt. If badly marked thay can be cleaned using a carpet shampoo. Remember that they must be dried thoroughly so choose your time for doing this. They may need drying overnight. Underfelt should be carefully shaken but not washed and beaten otherwise it will be difficult to dry and start to break up. If the carepting around the pedals is worn it is recommended that it be renewed as it can be a danger especially for lady drivers wearing heeled shoes.

When the carpeting is removed any water leaks will be evident and corrective action can be taken before rust sets in.

With a stiff handbrush or a vacuum cleaner with a flexible hose remove all traces of dust and grit that is left inside. For cleaning the upholstery materials and panels on the doors use a detergent liquid in a water solution. Do not overwet the areas being cleaned as you do not want interior padding to get soaked. It will smell or rot if it does. Stubborn marks or ingrained dirt should be shifted with a soft bristled brush. An old nailbrush is ideal.

When finished, wipe the surfaces as dry as possible and leave the windows open to air the car out. It is not advisable to do any interior car cleaning using water in wet weather - it takes too long to dry out.

When cleaning windows and screens use plain water and a chamois leather. A little household ammonia in the water prevents smears.

Never put damp carpets back in the car. If you are in a hurry to use the car leave them out until dry. Otherwise they will not dry properly and will get dirty again more quickly. They will deteriorate more quickly too.

Turning to the boot, remove the complete contents including spare wheel and vacuum out all the dust and dirt. Wipe the paintwork down with a damp cloth. If carpeting is fitted clean this as well in a similar manner to the interior carpeting. Again look for water leaks especially in the corners.

Should you have a slight tear on one of the seats or trim panel, cut a piece of spare trim from the underside of one of the seats and apply a coat of impact adhesive such as clear Bostik. Insert the patch into the hole with the glue uppermost and then apply adhesive to the flap of the torn section. Allow the recommended drying time to pass and then press down the torn edges trying to get the edges as close together as possible which will make the repair less pronounced. Any large tears will have to be repaired using a piece of matching material.

Car cleaning - exterior underside

It is recommended that if the car is in a dirty state it should be steam cleaned if possible. If it is not possible then you must prepare for a quite long and very dirty job.

You will need paraffin, water (preferably a hose) a wire brush, stiff bristle brush and a scraper.

Remove the carpets from the car and boot and jack up the car as high as possible at one end or at one side and take off the wheels that are raised. If you can jack up the whole car that will be best. Whatever you do, put double the quantity of blocks apparently necessary so that the car will not fall on you.

The first job is to scrape off that which can be scraped - this before sloshing any liquid about. Start from one end or one side and proceed methodically and particularly with the scraper and wire brush as appropriate. Coagulations of oily mud will clog the brush so try and scrape this and use the brush only for dry mud and awkward bits. Sweep up the scrapings and dispose of them before going to the next stage. Having scraped off all that can be scraped off the body floor should be washed off next with water - scrubbing as necessary with a bristle brush.

Do not use paraffin except in areas which are oil covered as this will make preparation of the surface for undersealing difficult. All mechanical parts which are not subject to rust can be flushed clean with paraffin using a brush and rag. Finally hose off and then examine the car interior to see what leaks there may be. This was the reason for removing the floor coverings. When dry plug the leaks from inside the car with a household sealant such as Seelastic. Check that outside all fittings, pipe clips, etc are secure before the underneath is painted. Explore the underneath for all hollow sections which might rust from the inside. If necessary, drill a hole into these and plug it later with the sealer.Spray into these hollow sections and into such places as the door interior an aerosol rust inhibitor, such as Supertrol 001, or Di-Nitrol 33B. These are thick and produce a protective jelly coating. Also spray this into awkward corners into which the underneath paint is going to be put in case penetration is not complete. The Supertrol 001 is also available in liquid form cheaper than an aerosol, and this will be cheaper for open patches of metal work that have been badly rusted. Now paint all parts of the underneath where there is either bare metal or unprotected ordinary paint, with an underneath paint. A thick, non-hard-setting material is needed. ADUP bronze superseal is recommended as it is compatible with the aerosols and so they 'wet' the metal and inhibit rust very thoroughly. Put thick layers of the paint where the wheels throw up stones.

Car cleaning - exterior

Once a week the exterior of the car should be washed and wiped dry. For this job a flexibrush on the end of the garden hose is ideal, a sponge to assist wiping down and a leather to finish the operation off.

First make sure that all windows and doors are closed. Thoroughly soak the car in water using a gentle spray. Once the dirt has been loosened by the water wipe down the panels using the brush with water still running through it - this way the paintwork should not be scratched by the dirt.

Next apply wax car shampoo or a little washing up liquid, working from the roof downwards. Any dead flies, marks or tar may be removed using a drop of paraffin on a cloth. Do not forget to clean the wing mirrors, front grille, the wiper arms and, of course, the wheels.

Finally rinse off with plenty of clean water and wipe dry using a leather. Bright work is cleaned in the same way. Occasionally one of the special polishes which can be obtained for chromium plating may be used but on no account use an ordinary metal polish.

Every six months it is recommended that the exterior be wax polished. There are, however, several important points to be noted before polish is used on a car.

1 If the paint is new do not polish for at least two months to allow the paint to dry fully and harden.

2 Do not use a 'cutting' paste to remove the dull film from cars which have been sprayed with a metallic paint.

3 When purchasing a wax plolish always make sure that it is suitable for the type of paintwork on the car.

4 Do not attempt to wax polish a car in the sun or when the body is still warm, having been in the sun. It will look awful and possibly damage the paint surface.

5 After washing the car make sure the surface is thoroughly dry before applying any polish. If it is a damp day wait for a dry one.

Finally, a few don'ts so as to avoid deterioration of the paintwork:

Don't dust or polish a dirty car. Always wash.

Don't get polish or wax on any of the glass.

Don't park under trees especially in the hot sun or when raining.

Don't use a cutting compound or haze remover on cars finished with an acrylic paint.

Bodywork – paint touch-up

Touch-up paint is usually available in a touch-up pencil, a tin with a little brush in the lid or aerosol form may be obtained as a good match to the original body colour. It must, however, be realised that some paint colours are more stable than others. Due to the action of sunlight on an older car an exact match may be difficult.

Use a touch-up tin with brush incorporated

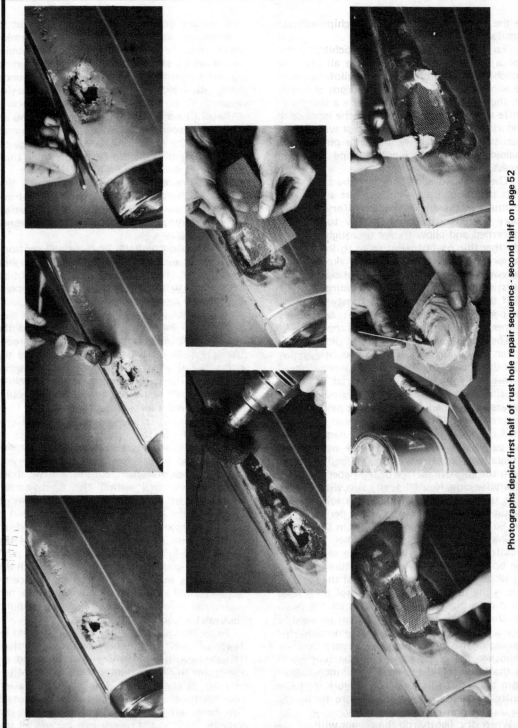

Photographs depict first half of rust hole repair sequence - second half on page 52

in the lid for making good stone chips and very small scratches.

To prepare the surface for touching-up first use a silicone solvent to remove all traces of polish which will otherwise not allow the paint to adhere properly. If there are signs of rusting or the paint beginning to lift use a sharp pen-knife and carefully scrape away the loose paint and rust. Then neutralise the rust with a little Kurust and allow to dry. With a piece of rag soaked in methylated spirits wipe away the excess.

The prepared spot may now be touched in with the touch-up brush. Use just sufficiently to touch in the area concerned. Very carefully apply a thin coat of paint only to the area concerned and allow to dry thoroughly. Apply a further thin coat of paint so as to build up to the original thickness. This will take time and patience but with care the touch-up should be indistinguishable from the surrounding area.

If there is a scratch on the paintwork which has penetrated the top coat of paint and the red primer is showing the procedure is the same.

The edges of doors and boot lid seem to suffer very much and small areas of rust frequently appear. In this case an aerosol tin of primer and top coat will be required, Again use the silicone solvent to remove any polish from the area concerned. Rub down the paint around the area with a little wet or dry paper grade 400 until the area is smooth. As the name implies the paper can be used with water without disintegrating. Water flushes the rubbed off paint from the abrasive surface of the paper. It would otherwise clog. Neutralise any rust with Kurust. It is useless trying to use an aerosol in damp conditions or anything other than perfectly still air. So choose a dry day and work in the garage.

Shake the aerosol tin of primer for a few minutes to ensure that there is no sediment in the bottom. Usually the manufacturer drops in a ball bearing to assist agitation of the paint. If this is the first time that an aerosol tin is used try it on a piece of metal such as an old tin to get the 'feel' of the spray and then proceed to spray the prepared surface. Remember the success of this work lies in the preparation. The smoother the prepared surface the better will be the finish. Hold the jet 8 to 12 inches away from the area to be sprayed and work from the centre outwards keeping the centre moist and the outside lightly sprayed and dry.

When dry, lightly rub the primer with wet or dry paper to roughen up the surface and inspect the surface for blemishes caused by dust or insufficient attention paid at the preparation stage. Rectify any faults found by rubbing down again and applying a further coat of primer. It is only when the surface under repair is perfect that the final top coat may be applied. Again experiment on an old piece of metal if this is your first time and when you are confident apply the top coat to the primer. Remember it is like ordinary household painting - two thin coats are better than one thick coat.

Should runs occur it is an indication that either too much paint has been applied at one go or the nozzle was too near to the surface being sprayed. Rub down the area concerned and start again.

With all touching-up, be it a small spot or a larger area, allow the paint to dry thoroughly, overnight at least, and then use a little rubbing compound to blend in the edges of the paint and remove any dry spray.

If the area is near to a piece of chrome trim there is no need to remove it. Mask up the chrome trim with a little sellotape or proper masking tape. This may be removed once the paint is half dry, leaving no paint overspray marks on the trim. Take care when sticking down the tape and pleat it if necessary around any curved areas.

Bodywork - deep scratching, dent or crease removal

This type of repair requires a little more work but is well within the do-it-yourself motorists' capabilities, provided that care is taken and the job is not rushed. Preparation is the secret to good results. The method of approach will depend on the location of the damage but in all cases if it is possible to push the dent or crease out from behind so much the better, This may mean removal of a piece of trim. Should this present problems do not worry too much provided you are able to build up to the original shape with filler.

Any damaged trim embellishment should be taken off and straightened separately. If their fixtures are broken they should be glued on later using a two part resin glue such as Araldite.

For safety reasons this next operation requires a pair if goggles or glasses to protect the eyes. Using an electric sander with an abrasive disc on the rubber pad remove all the paint right down to the bare metal from the

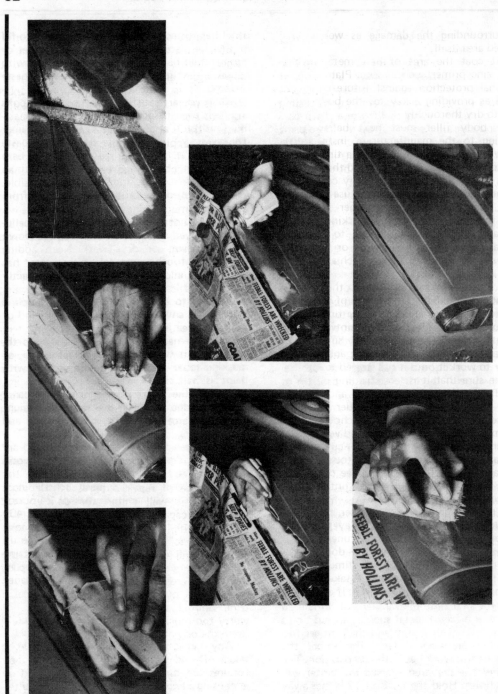

Photographs depict second half of rust hole repair sequence - first half on page 50

area surrounding the damage as well as the damaged area itself.

Next coat the area of bare metal with a speical zinc primer such as Zinc Plate to give additional protection against future corrosion as well as providing a key for the body filler. Allow to dry thoroughly.

The body filler must next be prepared according to the manufacturers' instructions. Usually these come in two parts, a tin of filler in paste form and a hardener. Read through the mixing instructions and when fully conversant mix only enough for immediate use to guard against waste. Once the hardener has been added the paste has a limited working time of only a few minutes. It is best to mix the material using a piece of plastic or very stiff cardboard on a smooth surface such as a glazed tile.

The filler should be applied to the damged area and about one inch either side of it so as to allow for preparing the surface for final finishing. Do not apply the filler to paintwork as it will not adhere properly. Carefully smooth the filler to the contour of the body panel, but do not try to work it once it has started to harden. Make sure that it is left standing proud to give adequate leeway for shaping and rubbing down. When dry the resin filler has the consistency of a hard bar of chocolate. A surform plane, dreadnought file and very coarse rasp are ideal tools to use for cutting the material down to the proper contour. As you get nearer to the final shape so the coarseness of the file should be reduced until finally abrasive paper may be used.

Do not use great lumps of filler in one go. Take your time and build up in layers, letting each layer harden in turn. Fill in uneven spots as and when needed. If you are doing a job using resin paste for the first time do not expect too much of yourself, it takes a little time to get the feel of the material. If an area of

panel has rusted out and you have a hole to fill in then a piece of perforated metal sheet or mesh should be attached behind the panel with adhesive or clips so that the resin filler paste can be built up on it, layer by layer.

When you are satisfied that the surface looks and feels even (it does not have to have a glass-like finish yet) apply a coat of cellulose primer (the grey one) to the whole area of filler paste and surround. This can go direct onto bare metal but it is best to cover bare metal with an under-primer such as Zinc Plate first if possible. This is supplied for brush application or from an aerosol.

Then add a normal primer. When the cellulose primer is dry it should be rubbed down with 400 wet or dry (wet). Keep adding another coat of primer (after the water has dried off) and rubbing down until a perfectly smooth finish is obtained.

The final colour coat may then be applied from the aerosol can. Do not spray in wind or direct sunlight.

If the area is a large one it may be worthwhile to spray the complete panel which, of course, should be rubbed down all over with 400 grade wet or dry (wet) first.

If you have colour sprayed part of a panel only leave it to harden for at least a fortnight before rubbing down with cutting paste and final polishing.

Aerosol paint sprays are expensive, and are not easy to use to give a final coat of a good surface. It is often quicker to brush on the paint. Use a slow drying thinner such as Belco. After the last coat has hardened for 24 hours, rub down with wet 'wet or dry' of grade 400 very lightly and with plenty of water. Just take off the top of the brush marks. Then shine up the paint with rubbing compound a fine cutting paste. Allow a further week for the paint to harden, then give a polish with car cleaner polish.

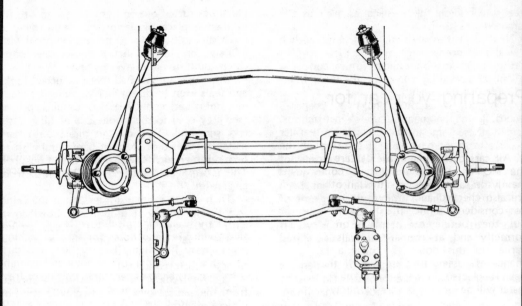

Steering mechanism and front suspension - plan view

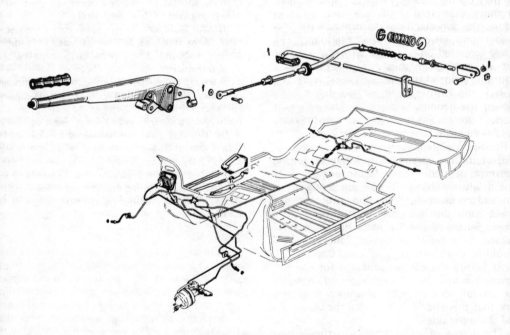

Layout of brake systems
Top - mechanical handbrake linkage: Bottom - hydraulic footbrake system

Preparing your car for the MOT Test

All cars over three years old are subject to the MOT test. The test itself concentrates mainly on safety asepcts although other points are also checked and may result in a failure if not considered serviceable. If you have carried out the routine maintenance on your car correctly and at regular intervals as shown earlier in this book you have a far better chance of passing the test than if the car has been neglected in any way. The points the tester will be looking for are as follows:

Steering

With the car standing on level ground check the play on the steering wheel. It should move no more than four inches at its outer edge before the wheels begin to move. Open the bonnet and check that the steering box is firmly mounted on the car and that there is no rust or rotting in this area weakening the mounting point of the steering box.

Jack the front of the car up, having first applied the handbrake and rock the wheels to check if there is any wear in the wheel bearings. Adjust them or renew as necessary as detailed in Routine Maintenance.

Rest the car on stacks or wooden blocks at the front, get under the car and check the tightness of all the linkages in the steering mechanism and check that all the nuts are tight and where applicable have their split pins correctly fitted. Excessive play or wear in any of the linkage may result in a test failure so this should be dealt with by your local Chrysler UK agent before the car is submitted for the test. Having lowered the car to the ground check the car on full lock in both directions and make sure that the wheels do not foul the bodywork and chafe the tyres.

The degree of wear allowed in the steering gear is not laid down precisely but it is up to the individual judgement of the tester as to whether he considers the car to be in a safe condition. Some testers may be more stringent than others but do not risk having a car with faulty steering; always have worn parts replaced as a matter of course.

Brakes

Carefully examine all the metal and flexible hydraulic pipes and hoses for signs of leaking, corrosion and chafing. Clean off the mud, dirt, etc from the flexible rubber hoses and examine them for any signs of perishing, bulging or fraying caused by rubbing or stones thrown up.

Check round the brake drums for any sign of hydraulic fluid leakage from the wheel cylinders. This form of leakage will severely affect braking efficiency when the car is road tested.

Get in the car, release the handbrake and depress the brake pedal. If there is excessive travel on the pedal before the brakes operate, the brakes will need adjusting. If there is evidence of sponginess in the pedal it will mean that air has entered the hydraulic system and the brakes will need bleeding. Both these tasks are covered in this handbook.

Check that the handbrake cable is in good condition and that the clevis pins on the rear brake backplates are not worn and their retaining split pins are in place. Check that the handbrake operates correctly. When the brakes are correctly adjusted the handbrake should travel up the ratchet about four or five clicks to be fully on.

Lights

Switch on all the lights and check that they are all functioning correctly. Check the operation of the headlamps on full beam and dipped beam. Also check that the main beam warning light operates when the lights are on full beam.

Back the car up against a wall and check that the brake stop lights work both with and without the tail lights on in the reflection.

Check the operation of the indicator lights both front and rear. They should flash at between 50 and 120 times per minute.

Check that the lenses of the tail and brake lights are not broken or faded; they must show a positive, bold red light.

Bodywork and underframe
The tester will examine the car thoroughly for excessive signs of rust and corrosion, particularly where the corrosion points may affect the safety of the car, such as rear spring mounting points, front suspension strut top mountings visible under the bonnet, steering box mounting point etc.

Exhaust system
An exhaust system must be leakproof and keep engine noise below a level of 86 decibels. Leaks may cause dangerous fumes to enter the interior and affect the driver and passengers - thus having an adverse effect on the driver's capabilities. Excessive noise constitutes a public nuisance. Both these faults can result in the vehicle being declared unfit for use.

Windscreen washers and wipers
It is now a legal requirement for vehicles to be fitted with windscreen washers. Ensure that both wipers and washers are working satisfactorily.

Seat belts
Safety checks on seat belts are dealt with in the General Information section of this handbook.

Road test
The purpose of the tester driving the car on the road is to ensure himself that it handles properly. If there is anything major wrong with the steering, you will probably already have spotted this fault and had it rectified before the test.

The tester will check the efficiency of the brakes by using a decelerometer, a piece of equipment which is not readily available to the public. However, you can do a rough test on the brakes by using an ordinary brick. Get the car onto a reasonably long, deserted, straight and smooth piece of road, place the brick on the front passenger floor on one of its narrow longer sides and gently accelerate up to 30 mph. Checking that it is safe to do so, apply the brakes hard without actually locking the wheels. The brick should fall over at this point quite quickly. Repeat the test and stop the car using the handbrake only; this time the brick should just topple over quite gently.

If the car pulls violently to one side or the other on heavy braking this may well cause a failure of the test. Refer in this case to the fault finding tables.

Conclusion
If all appears to be well the car can now be submitted for its test. Before taking it in make sure you have the log book and the old test certificate to hand for the tester. Have enough petrol in the tank to enable the road test to be carried out.

It is advisable to leave instructions with the garage telling them that should any minor faults be found they should be put right on the spot to prevent a further waste of time and money. Any major faults should be told to you before the repair work is begun. If your car fails its test because of a fault of this nature do not get upset about it. Remember that the tester is thinking of your safety and the safety of other road users and be thankful that any fault was discovered before it may have caused an accident.

Buying and selling a used Car

When you are looking for a car in this range do not look at any one in detail till you have seen a number to get a feel of the sort of prices being asked for cars in various conditions. In the guide that follows various things to look for are listed. Very likely your car will have some of the defects you look out for. You will not find a perfect car. The object is to find out what faults the car has so you know what has to be done to it before it is usable, what is likely to go wrong soon after, and what sort of bills you will have to meet in the first few months of ownership.

Walk round the car a few yards away from it and see if it sits evenly on the ground.

Does the paintwork on the body panels match up perfectly? If not the car has probably been in an accident.

If you suspect respraying check closely round the chrome strips and windscreen rubbers to see if there is any evidence of paint on them.

If you suspect signs of filler a good way of checking this is to run along the suspect area with a magnet. The magnet will not grip on areas which have been filled.

Check the operation and tight fitting of the doors, boot lid and bonnet.

Look for signs of rust round the wings, sills, particularly the area of the front wings (particularly the inner wings) etc and for any signs of paintwork bubbling. This will indicate rust coming through from underneath which may have been covered up by a quick spray but which will eat its way through again very quickly.

Look at the condition of the upholstery in the car, even when the seats have been covered. This will give a fair idea as to the way the car was treated by its previous owner. Also look at the wear on the carpets and, if not replaced, the pedal rubbers. Replacement too indicates age.

Whilst in the car try the handbrake to see if it is correctly adjusted, the footbrake and clutch to check the pedal travel and free movement. Move the gear stick into all positions to see if it is positive and precise.

Get out of the car and open the bonnet. Have a thorough check round the engine compartment for signs of either oil or water leaks. Remove the dipstick and check the colour and level of the oil. If it is very black it will need changing. If there is evidence, by feeling grittiness and faint traces of white metal in the oil the engine is probably badly worn.

Check the condition of all ignition HT leads. If they are cracked they will need renewing at an early date. Check that the distributor and its cap are firm and not damaged in any way.

Ask someone to start the engine and have a look at the colour of the exhaust gases. If it is very smoky or blue this indicates considerable wear in the engine. The colour of the interior of the exhaust pipe outlet will only be indicative if the car has been run for at least 10 miles before looking at it. Basically it should be light grey in colour - black and sooty may indicate a tired engine.

Listen to the engine while it is running. There should be no prominent taps or rattles of any kind. When the engine is revved up suddenly there should be no evidence of any excessive noise other than normal engine noise; any heavy thumping at this stage may indicate worn big end bearings.

Turning to the electrical system check that all the lights, including the indicators, work correctly and are consistently bright and do not fluctuate in intensity with engine speed. Check that the ignition warning light goes out immediately the engine speed is increased from idling.

Having a good look round the battery for signs of seepage, cracking, etc and check the condition of the battery terminals.

Check the top of the front suspension mountings and rear spring mountings for rust.

Walk round the car again and examine the state of the tyres. Check that, if worn, they have

Hillman Hunter Deluxe Saloon

Hillman Hunter GL Estate

done so evenly. If they have worn unevenly or show signs of scuffing there possibly may be something wrong with the suspension geometry or the steering. Also check the condition of the spare and ensure that it is inflated. Whilst checking the spare, make sure that there is a jack and a wheel brace of the correct type for the car.

Try to rock the front wheels, both vertically and horizontally. Any movement may indicate maladjusted front wheel bearings or wear in the steering linkage.

Get back in the car and check how much movement there is on the steering wheel rim before the wheels move. There should not be more than two inches as an absolute maximum. Any more than this indicates wear in the linkage.

Check the condition of the shock absorbers by bouncing the car on its suspension at all four corners. Good shock absorbers will return the car to rest almost immediately; with worn shock absorbers the car will continue to bounce for a second or so.

Having checked all these points, tell the seller of the car that you would like a road test (this is not possible at car auctions). Do not immediately drive the car yourself, but spend the first few minutes in checking a few more points such as the interior noise level, excessive transmission noise, clonks on taking up the drive indicating worn universal joints or back axle.

When you start driving yourself check the following points:
a) Does the car steer well without wandering and too much correcting?
b) Is the gearbox smooth and does the synchromesh operate well without crunching the gears?
c) Try the brakes, first gently then hard, warning your passenger of your intention to do so. Do they pull the car up quickly, without judder and without pulling the car to one side?

Once your road test has been completed open the bonnet again and check that there still are no signs of leaking oil and water.

If you want to make sure you are paying a reasonable price for the car it is worth purchasing a copy of the 'Motorists Guide to New and Used Car Prices' which is published monthly and can be found on most bookstalls. It gives a very fair assessment as to the value of a used car, according to model, year, condition,

etc. The decision to buy or not now rests with you.

Selling

Much of what has been said with regard to buying a used car is relevant in selling one except, of course, that the boot is on the other foot.

Whatever the reasons are for selling, be they that you want a bigger, better or different car, you simply need the money, or your circumstances have changed, there is the relatively simple, standard approach - you want the best price for your car. With this end in view, whilst we hope that you will be giving value for money at the same time, a basic method of preparation for the car exists. Cleanliness is all. The cleaner the car, the higher the price. The bodywork's condition, both inside and out, is usually the main selling point. Mechanical repair work is often cheaper and faster to undertake than extensive bodywork repairs or renovation. The condition of the bodywork is usually indicative of the total condition of the car because it will show signs of age and disrepair sooner than the engine or gearbox, particularly on cars more than three years old. It is unlikely that owners will keep their cars in excellent condition mechanically and allow the body to drop off around it. Attend to the paintwork, chrome and all exterior trim, clean the outside thoroughly and polish the car, clean out the boot, the engine compartment and 'spring clean' the interior. Methods of doing this are explained in the Bodywork Chapter of this book. Because of the short time usually taken to actually complete a sale there can only be something less than a complete detailed check by a potential purchaser and rather more, a quick visual one.

As there are various ways of buying a used car so there are similar methods of selling but they are considered on their merits from completely different standpoints. The way in which you sell your car will depend on why you are selling. The best prices are often obtained when part exchanging your car for a new one from an accredited dealer. However, shop around from dealer to dealer; their buying-in-prices will vary according to how eager they are to sell the new car you want, and how eager they are to have your present car to re-sell. Nevertheless, with many dealers not wanting used cars of more than three years old it may be better to sell privately whatever your circumstances. Here, local papers, notice boards etc are the best media.

It is unlikely that you will receive the best price from a used car dealer at least as a cash transaction, unless he requires a good example for a particular customer, because he will have to put his mark-up onto the car to re-sell. Auctions do not often provide the best recompense. You can, of course, put a reserve price. They usually do provide a sale though, if you are finding it difficult to sell your particular car.

The same premise applies when you are selling your car as when you are buying one with regard to the actual selling price. The same guide is valid. However, these are other indications. Go around to various dealers and ask them for the prices of used cars of a similar age and condition to yours and look at the prices in the local papers, and then fix a reasonable price and be prepared to bargain. There are obviously price trends with regard to time and place to sell. Prices usually creep upwards in the spring and you may be fortunate enough to live in a high demand area such as London or eastern England where prices will again be marginally higher than elsewhere.

Remember when selling your car that the law exists both to protect you and the buyer. The Trades Description Act does affect you as the seller. If the car you are selling is under a hire purchase agreement, the permission of the finance company must be obtained first. Irrespective of the age of your car it must have a current road fund licence, MOT certificate (when applicable) and insurance before it can even be tested on the road. Always give a receipt and do not part with the car and log book until you are sure you have the money if you are paid by cheque. Do not forget to make sure your name is removed from the log book, and the buyer's inserted and that the local Taxation Office is informed of a change of ownership.

Arrows indicate potential rusting points

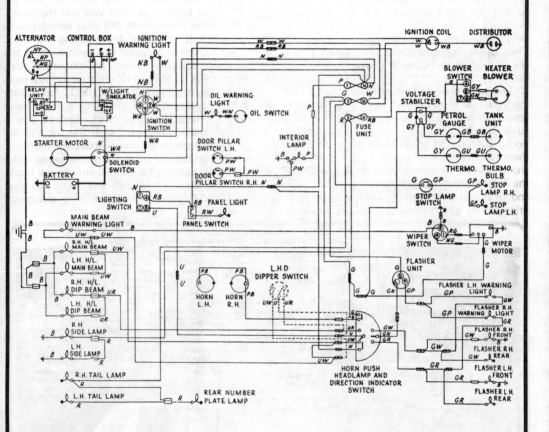

Hillman Hunter - wiring diagram
Early model

COLOUR CODE		ABBREVIATIONS
R	RED	N	BROWN	R.H. = RIGHT-HAND
Y	YELLOW	P	PURPLE	L.H. = LEFT-HAND
G	GREEN	W	WHITE	L.H.D. = LEFT-HAND DRIVE
U	BLUE	B	BLACK	H/L = HEADLAMP

SYMBOLS	
-------	ALTERNATIVE WIRING FOR LEFT-HAND DRIVE MODELS
	SNAP CONNECTOR
	PLUG AND SOCKET CONNECTOR
	EARTH THROUGH CABLE
●	EARTH THROUGH UNIT

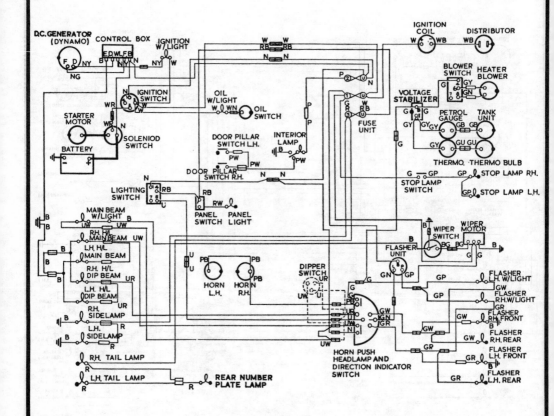

Hillman Minx - wiring diagram
Early model

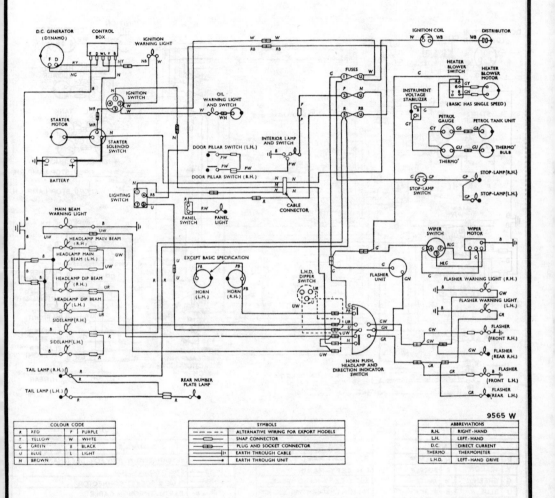

Hillman Minx Saloon and Estate - wiring diagram
From chassis No. BO 11064891 Saloon; BO 081011551 Estate

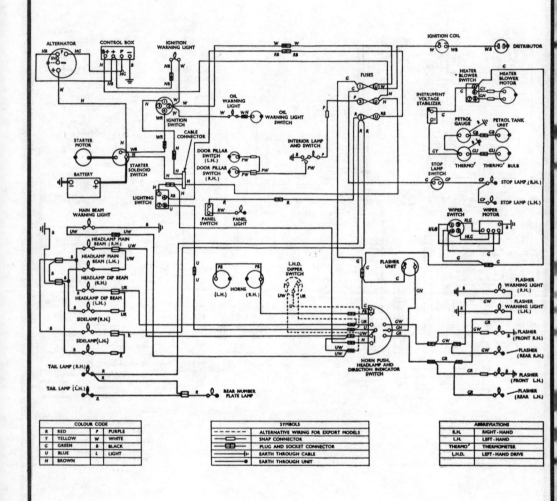

Hillman Hunter - wiring diagram
From chassis No. BO 52017039

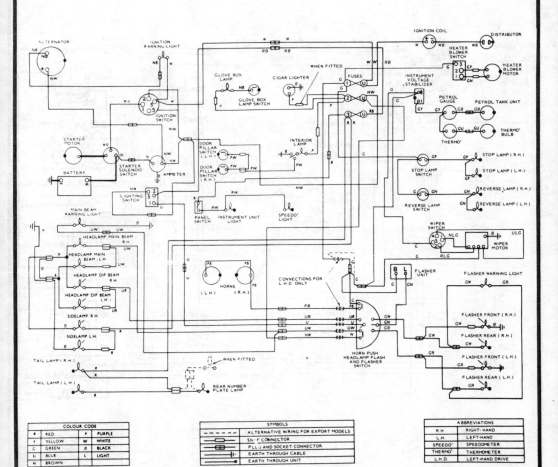

Hillman Hunter GL Saloon and GL Estate - wiring diagram
From chassis No. LH0597 Saloon; LH 1507 Estate

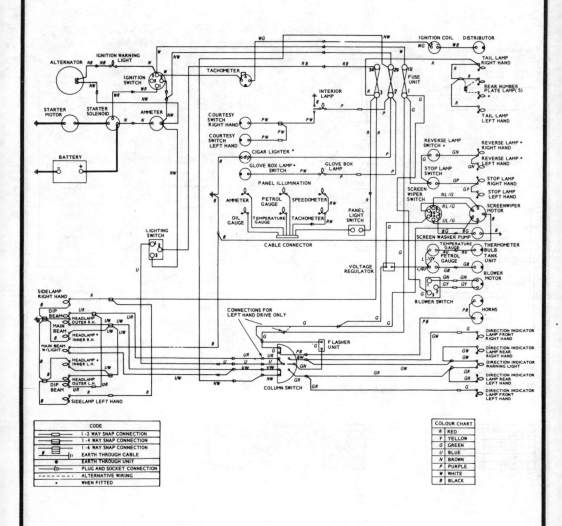

Hillman Hunter GLS and GT - wiring diagram
From chassis No. LH0407 GLS; LH0317 GT

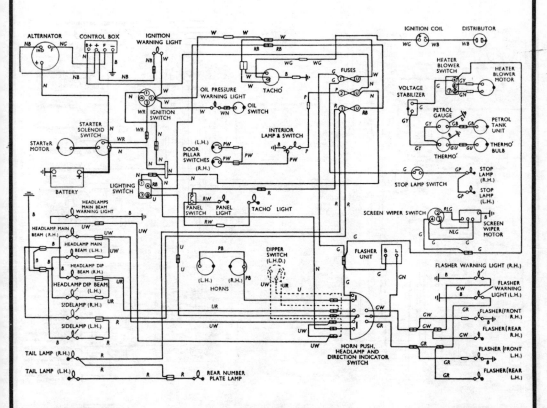

Hillman GT - wiring diagram

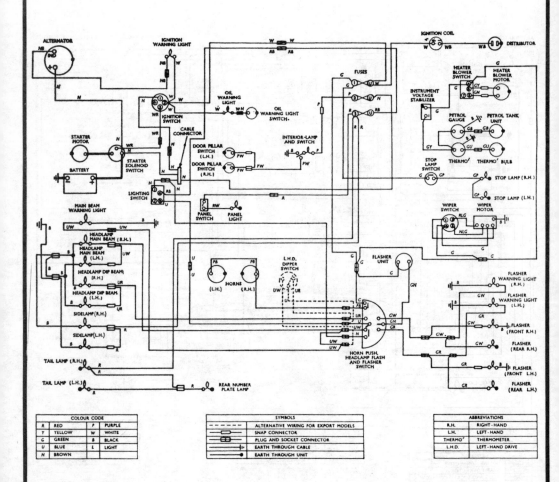

Hillman Hunter - wiring diagram
Models fitted with 16ACR alternators

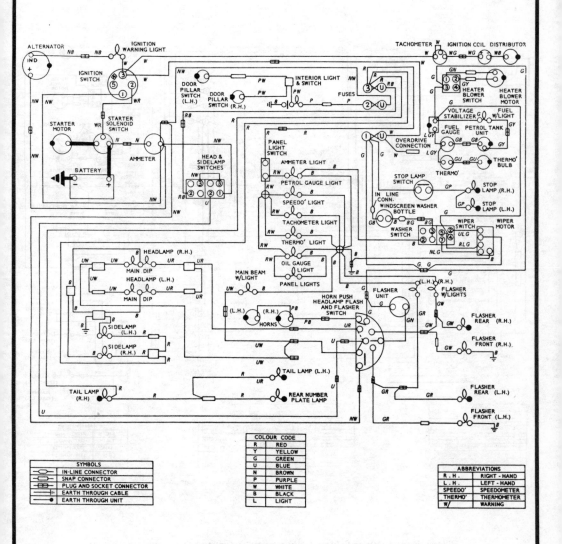

Hillman Hunter GT - wiring diagram
From chassis No. L G 830600001

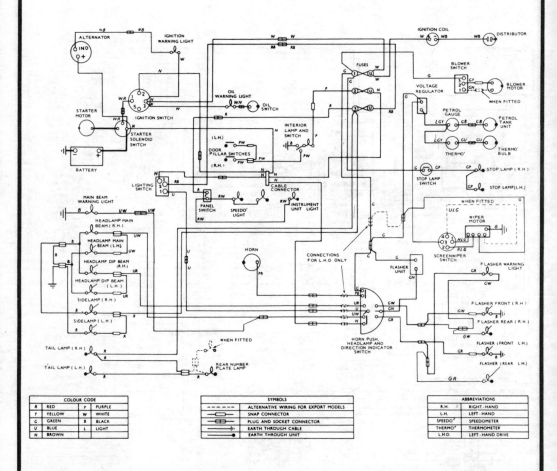

Hillman Hunter Deluxe Saloon, Deluxe Estate and Hunter Super - wiring diagram
From chassis No. LH 0647 Deluxe Saloon; LH 1607 Deluxe Estate;
LH 0757 Super

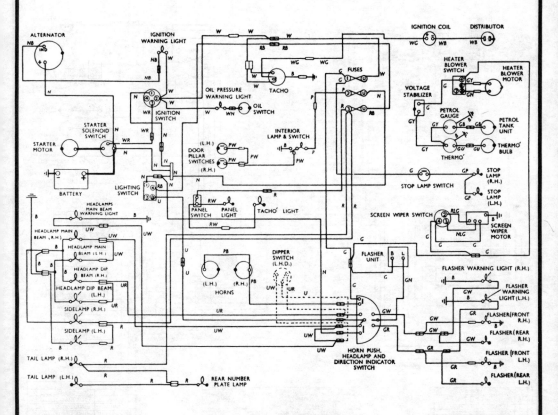

Hillman GT - wiring diagram
Models fitted with 16 ACR alternators

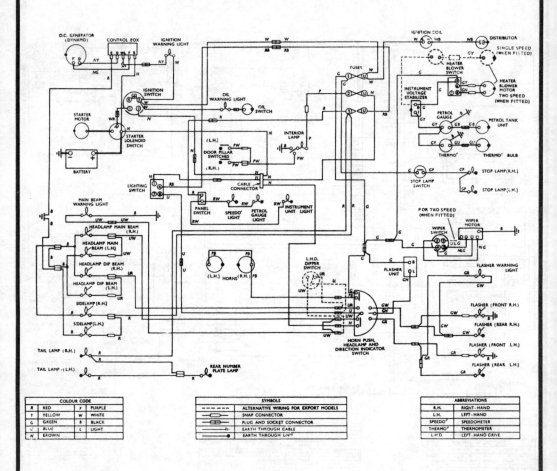

Hillman Hunter Deluxe Saloon, Deluxe Estate and Hunter Super - wiring diagram
From chassis No. L G 063600001 Deluxe Saloon; L G 085600001 Deluxe Estate; L G 074600001 Super

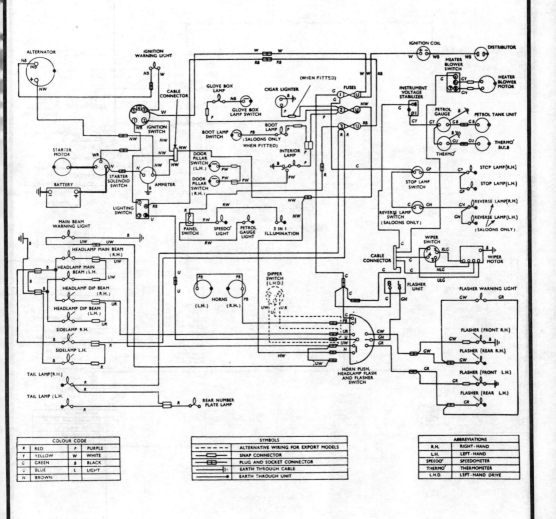

Hillman Hunter GL Saloon and Estate - wiring diagram
From chassis No. LG 058600001 Saloon; LG 087600001 Estate

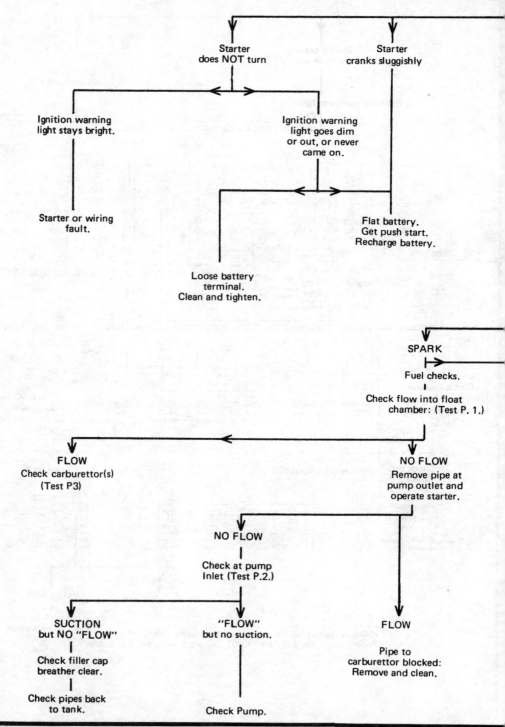

Starter
does NOT turn

Starter
cranks sluggishly

Ignition warning
light stays bright.

Ignition warning
light goes dim
or out, or never
came on.

Starter or wiring
fault.

Flat battery.
Get push start.
Recharge battery.

Loose battery
terminal.
Clean and tighten.

SPARK

Fuel checks.

Check flow into float
chamber: (Test P. 1.)

FLOW
Check carburettor(s)
(Test P3)

NO FLOW
Remove pipe at
pump outlet and
operate starter.

NO FLOW

Check at pump
Inlet (Test P.2.)

SUCTION
but NO "FLOW"

"FLOW"
but no suction.

FLOW

Check filler cap
breather clear.

Pipe to
carburettor blocked:
Remove and clean.

Check pipes back
to tank.

Check Pump.

Stoppages

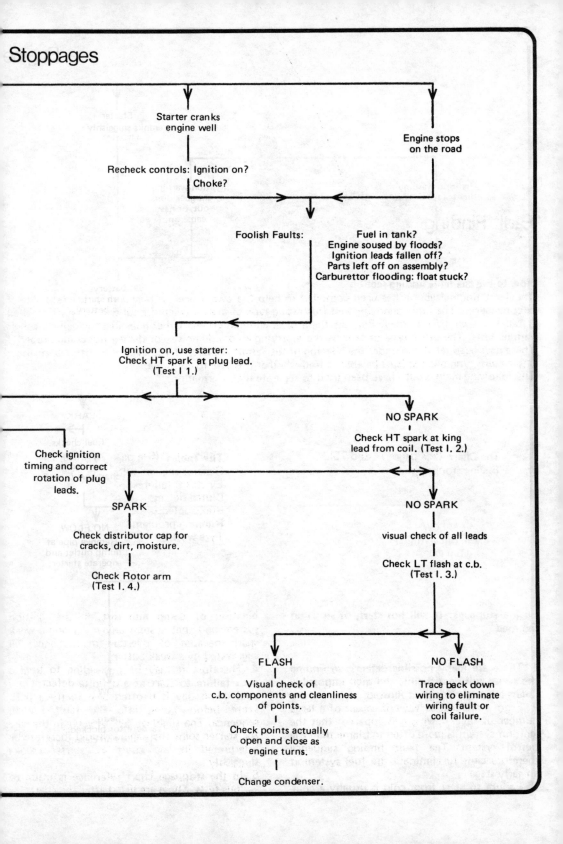

Starter cranks
engine well

Engine stops
on the road

Recheck controls: Ignition on?
Choke?

Foolish Faults:

Fuel in tank?
Engine soused by floods?
Ignition leads fallen off?
Parts left off on assembly?
Carburettor flooding: float stuck?

Ignition on, use starter:
Check HT spark at plug lead.
(Test I 1.)

NO SPARK

Check HT spark at king
lead from coil. (Test I. 2.)

Check ignition
timing and correct
rotation of plug
leads.

SPARK

Check distributor cap for
cracks, dirt, moisture.

Check Rotor arm
(Test I. 4.)

NO SPARK

visual check of all leads

Check LT flash at c.b.
(Test I. 3.)

FLASH

Visual check of
c.b. components and cleanliness
of points.

Check points actually
open and close as
engine turns.

Change condenser.

NO FLASH

Trace back down
wiring to eliminate
wiring fault or
coil failure.

Fault Finding

How to use the fault finding section

The fault finding section has been compiled to help the owner deal with two very different sets of circumstances. The most annoying and frustrating type of fault is when the car will not start or when it breaks down on a journey. For this there is an elimination chart that goes methodically through various tests. The other type of fault is the worrying kind; odd noises, or the car not going properly. These have been tabulated under the heading of the symptom. Even if you cannot rectify one of these latter faults, you must at least be able to find whether it is safe to continue.

The following main groups have been used to separate the information:

The Chart (See pages 74 and 75)
Engine stoppages

The Tables (See page 78 onwards)
General engine faults
Electrical failures
Clutch defects
Brake defects
Running problems
Tyre wear

Engine stoppage: It will not start, or stops on the road

1 There are many possible defects, so finding the cause will be difficult, and nigh impossible unless a logical course is followed.

2 From statistical surveys of causes of a large number of breakdowns, it is apparent that the ignition system is more often to blame than the petrol system. The fault finding sequence therefore aims to eliminate the fuel system at an early stage.

3 Failure to start from cold is usually a com- bination of damp and dirt on the ignition system and that system anyway giving a weak spark because of overdue maintenance, all aggravated by a weak battery.

4 Therefore it may be misleading to treat a car's failure to start as a definite defect. On a cold damp day it is often best to try a push start before going into the fault finding sequence. The slightest lack of verve in the way the starter spins the engine should therefore be interpreted in the chart as 'starter cranks sluggishly'.

5 In the stoppage chart reference is made to various tests. These are listed after the chart.

TESTS OF THE IGNITION SYSTEM

Test I.1

Check ignition HT at a plug

a) Switch on ignition
b) Take an HT lead off a plug
c) Hold metal contact of the fitting on the end of the lead 1/8 inch from a bright metal 'earth' such as the cylinder head. If the plug lead fitting has a shroud to cover the plug, stick a ¼ inch bolt into the contact as a probe.
d) Operate the starter
e) There should be an easily noticeable spark.

Test I.2

Ignition HT at source

a) If possible take the central, King, lead from the distributor cap and hold it 1/8 inch from earth and repeat as for test 1.
b) If the king lead is not readily detachable from the distributor cap, remove it from the coil and rig up a temporary lead.

Test I.3

Check ignition LT at contact breaker

a) Remove the distributor cap
b) Ignition switch on
c) Open contact breaker points with a thin screwdriver or if the engine has stopped so that they are already open, short them with the screwdriver
d) There should be a small but definite spark.

Test I.4

Check the rotor arm

a) This test is to see if there is a short through the body of the rotor arm to the spindle beneath
b) Rig up the king lead as for test 1.2, or a substitute lead
c) But hold the lead, not to the block, but near the centre of the metal contact on the top of the rotor arm
d) Operate the starter
e) There should be only one small spark as the metallic mass of the rotor arm contact is electrically charged and then no further sparks
f) Continuous sparks mean there is current flow to somewhere; thus a faulty rotor arm

TESTS OF THE PETROL SYSTEM

Test P.1

Fuel flow into carburettor

a) Remove the fuel pipe where it enters the carburettor
b) Operate the starter to work the meachanical petrol pump. Take care the pipe is not pointed at ignition leads or a hot exhaust pipe
c) Fuel should gush out of the pipe.

Test P.2

Check fuel flow into the pump

a) This is difficult to check as the pump draws fuel up by suction
b) Remove the pipe into the pump from the tank
c) Suck on the end of the pipe and find if petrol can be drawn up, but beware petrol does not get into the mouth. Ideally lengthen the pipe with some clear plastic tubing so that the flow of petrol can be seen coming. If by mischance fuel gets into the mouth spit it out at once, cough and spit some more
d) If petrol can not be drawn up by sucking try blowing. Have an assistant listen at the tank for the bubbling of the blowing. If there is resistance at first, and then it eases, it could be that the blowing has pushed out a blockage.
e) Also whilst the pipe is off the pump inlet, work the starter with a finger over the inlet union. The suction of the pump should be felt.

Test P.3

Carburettor check

a) Stromberg carburettors. Raise the air valve piston by means of the lifting pin (this is beneath the depression chamber cover on the right hand side of the carburettor) and listen to hear if the piston falls when the pin is released quickly
b) Weber carburettors. Remove the float chamber covers of each carburettor in turn. Remove jets one at a time and check for contamination.

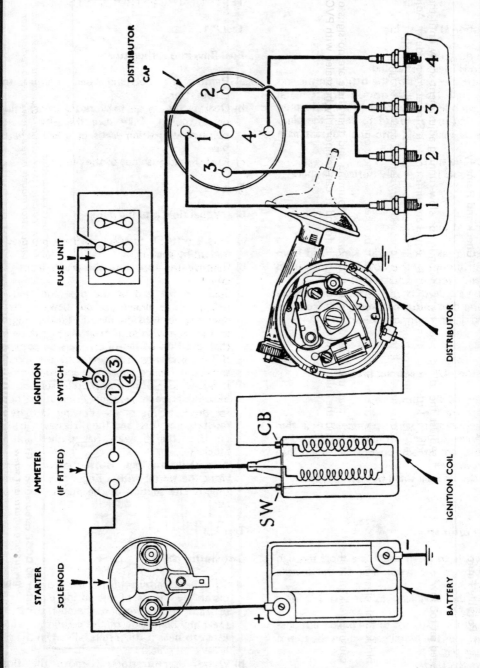

Diagram illustrating the circuitry of a typical ignition system
LT (primary) circuit - thin lines; HT circuit - heavy lines

Symptom Engine stalls when idling or has very rough idle

Possible Fault	Check and Remedy
Idling speed set too low	Adjust the idling speed by screwing in the slow-running adjustment screw until the engine idles a little faster. (Both screws by equal amounts on twin Stromberg models). Adjustment to the mixture controls is not recommended and if the above fails to rectify the fault it is recommended that the advice of an approved Chrysler UK agent is sought.
Dirty or blocked air cleaner.	Check the air cleaner. If the element is blocked, fit a new one.
Air leak causing weak mixture	Check that the carburettor is tight on its mounting and that there are no signs of cracks round the inlet manifold. If a crack is found it can temporarily be sealed with PVC tape or similar material but a professional repair will have to be carried out very soon.
Dirty plugs or incorrect gap	Remove the plugs, clean them and check the gaps.
Contact breaker points dirty, incorrectly set or worn	Thoroughly check the points as described in the 5,000 service schedule, Item 10.3

Stromberg carburettor
Arrow indicates slow running adjustment screw. Twin carburettor models have a screw on each carburettor

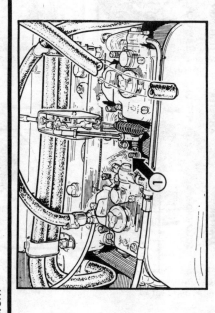

Weber 40 DCOE carburettors — GLS only
1 Slow running adjustment screw

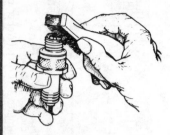

Cleaning deposits from electrodes and surrounding area using a fine wire brush.

Checking plug gap with feeler gauges

Altering the plug gap. Note use of correct tool.

Spark plug maintenance

White deposits and damaged porcelain insulation indicating overheating

Broken porcelain insulation due to bent central electrode

Electrodes burnt away due to wrong heat value or chronic pre-ignition (pinking)

Excessive black deposits caused by over-rich mixture or wrong heat value

Mild white deposits and electrode burnt indicating too weak a fuel mixture

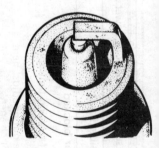

Plug in sound condition with light greyish brown deposits

Spark plug electrode conditions

General Engine Faults

Symptom Engine suffers from lack of power and acceleration

Possible Fault	Check and Remedy
Air cleaner dirty or blocked	If blocked fit a new element.
Incorrect setting of ignition timing	See ignition timing under 'Other Maintenance'.
Accelerator linkage out of adjustment	Check that full travel of the pedal gives full travel of the accelerator linkage at the carburettor.
Insufficient fuel reaching the engine	See P1, P2 and P3 under 'Engine Stoppage' in this Section.
Valve clearances incorrect	Check and adjust the valve to rocker arm clearance as described in the 5000 service schedule.
Automatic advance in distributor incorrect	This is not a fault that is easily diagnosed. Take your car to your local dealer for a proper check.
Engine compression low due to burnt valves	Once again this will have to be properly checked by your local garage. If the valves are burnt, the cylinder head will have to be removed and the valves reground.

Symptom Engine misfires at higher revs

Possible Fault	Check and Remedy
Loose or corroded electrical contacts in ignition system	Check, clean and tighten down all connections on the battery, coil and distributor. Check the condition of all leads. If they are cracked or damaged replace them as they may well be shorting under certain conditions.
Spark plugs dirty, gaps incorrect or plugs need replacement	Remove the plugs, clean them thoroughly, check they are the right type, and examine them for signs of damage. If all is well regap the plugs and replace them.
Points dirty, burnt or gap incorrectly set	Thoroughly check over the points, clean them, and adjust the gap as described in the 5000 service schedule, Item 10.3.
Dirt or water in carburettor	Clean the carburettor and blow out the jets to remove all sediment and dirt (Weber carburettors only).

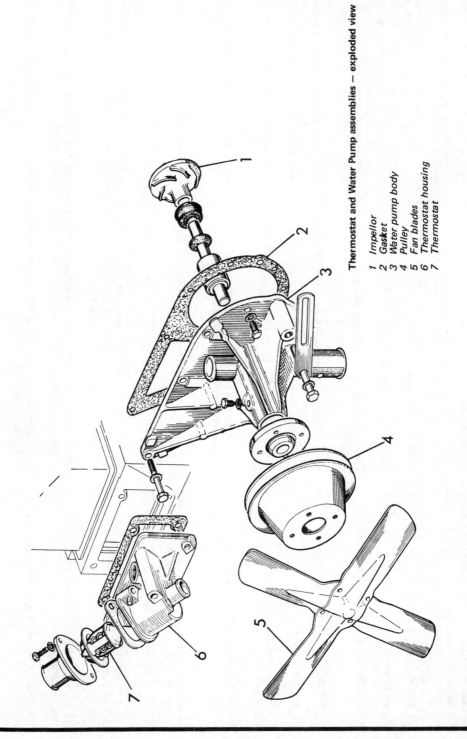

Thermostat and Water Pump assemblies — exploded view

1 Impellor
2 Gasket
3 Water pump body
4 Pulley
5 Fan blades
6 Thermostat housing
7 Thermostat

General Engine Faults

Symptom Engine overheats when running under normal conditions

Possible Fault	Check and Remedy
Lack or loss of coolant	If coolant is boiling, switch off the engine and wait for some ten minutes until it has stopped. Then carefully remove the radiator cap with a large rag. As the system is under pressure the hot coolant may shoot out and if care is not taken a nasty burn could result. Whilst waiting for things to cool down a bit have a good look round all hoses, hose connections, drain taps, the radiator and the heater for signs of a leak. A leak is very often apparent by signs of rust, water or antifreeze but this can be misleading if the leaking coolant has been blown around by the fan. If it is apparent that one or more of the hoses are defective these will have to be replaced eventually but a short distance can be covered by wrapping the defective spot with tape and running with the radiator cap off to prevent the coolant being forced out of the leak under pressure. Do not top up the cooling system until it has cooled down for at least 30 minutes, or cold water going in may cause the metal in the block and head to contract too fast and crack. Should it be established that the radiator has a leak this is a slightly more difficult problem if far from home. If a can of Radweld is kept in the car, top up the coolant to within about an inch of the top of the radiator (re-warm the engine to ensure the thermostat is open), pour in the Radweld, refit the radiator cap and rev the engine a few times to let the Radweld circulate and be drawn into the leakage area and effect a seal. Any temporary measure used; the radiator should be removed and repaired by an expert as soon as it is practical. A bad leak can be temporarily patched with the 'plastic padding' if the coolant is drained below the level of the leak till the plastic sets.
Loose or broken fan belt	At the same time check that the fan belt is in position and the tension is correct as shown in the service schedule. Adjust the tension if necessary. If it is broken and you have a replacement in the car, put it on. If not a temporary belt can be rigged up with a nylon stocking or one half of a pair of nylon tights. This will not last long but will probably enable you to get to a garage without too much overheating.
Thermostat stuck in closed position	Remove the thermostat housing and lift out the thermostat. If the engine is very hot and the thermostat is closed, Remove it and at a later date replace it with a new one. The thermostat housing is immediately behind the fan.
Blocked radiator either internally or externally	If the radiator fins are blocked with foreign matter this should be washed out with a pressure hose to allow the air to flow freely round the fins and do an effective cooling job. If a lot of oil is mixed in with the foreign matter the best way to move this is to take the car to your local garage and have the radiator steam cleaned. With time the cooling system may lose its efficiency as rust scales, hard water deposits and other sediment build up in the radiator and

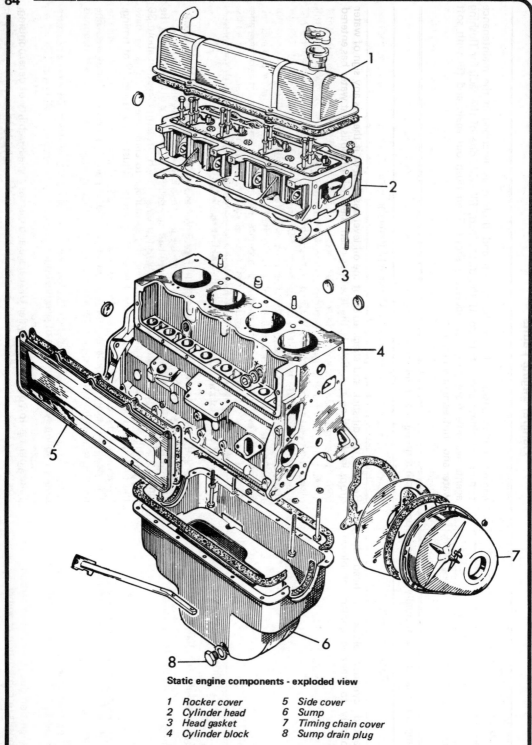

Static engine components - exploded view

1	Rocker cover	5	Side cover
2	Cylinder head	6	Sump
3	Head gasket	7	Timing chain cover
4	Cylinder block	8	Sump drain plug

General Engine Faults

engine cooling passages. Drain the system and flush it as described in the maintenance section for filling and antifreeze. If the dirt is bad, fill with one of the radiator flushing agents available from garages or accessory shops. Then flush out again and fill with soft water and antifreeze or an inhibitor.

Symptom Radiator continually requires topping up but no signs of external leakage

Possible Fault	Check and Remedy
Cracked cylinder block or head due probably to freezing coolant or blown cylinder head gasket	Remove the dipstick and check to see if the oil level has risen or if there is any sign of water drops in the oil on the stick. If the level has risen then it is obvious that water has entered the sump and the oil is floating on the top of it. After the engine has been running for some time in this condition the oil on the dipstick may appear to be milky in colour. Oil will probably also have found its way into the cooling system and this can be seen by a film of oil floating on top of the coolant in the radiator. A leaking head or block may also be accompanied by the discharge of excessive amounts of steam from the exhaust pipe, even when the engine is thoroughly warmed up.

Symptom Engine 'pinks' under acceleration

Possible Fault	Check and Remedy
Too low octane fuel being used	On next fill up use one star higher grade of fuel and check to see if this eliminates 'pinking'.
Ignition timing too far advanced	Check the timing. Excessive 'pinking' can damage the engine. It is well worth retarding the ignition slightly by turning the knurled vernier adjuster in the 'R' (retard) direction about 30 clicks until the 'pinking' is eliminated. Even if you manage to eliminate the 'pinking' have the timing checked as soon as possible. Eleven clicks on the adjuster represents 1° of timing.
Faulty automatic advance mechanism in distributor	This fault will only become apparent when the ignition timing has been correctly set. The remedy of it is best left to your local Chrysler UK garage as it will need electronic diagnosis equipment to check.
Pre-ignition due to engine overheating	Check cooling system for signs of overheating.
Pre-ignition due to excessive carbon deposits in combustion chamber	Take your car to your local Chrysler UK garage and discuss the advisability of decarbonising.

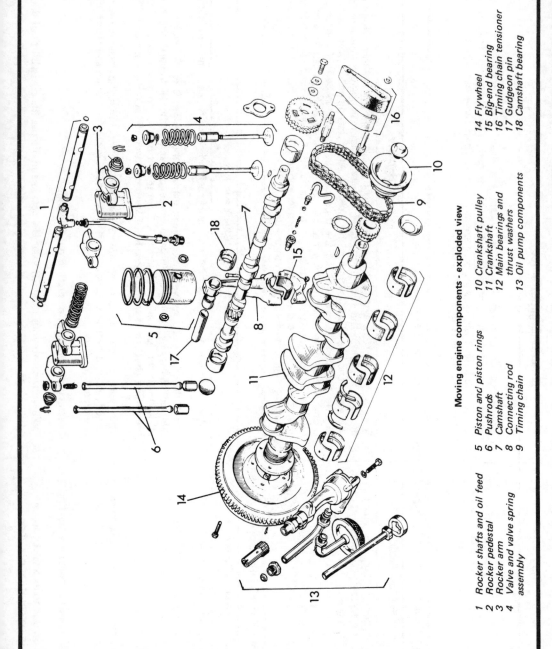

Moving engine components - exploded view

1 Rocker shafts and oil feed
2 Rocker pedestal
3 Rocker arm
4 Valve and valve spring
   assembly

5 Piston and piston rings
6 Pushrods
7 Camshaft
8 Connecting rod
9 Timing chain

10 Crankshaft pulley
11 Crankshaft
12 Main bearings and
    thrust washers
13 Oil pump components

14 Flywheel
15 Big-end bearing
16 Timing chain tensioner
17 Gudgeon pin
18 Camshaft bearing

General Engine Faults

Symptom Engine suffers from excessive oil consumption

Possible Fault	Check and Remedy
Oil leaks from crankshaft rear oil seal, timing cover gasket and oil seal, rocker cover gasket, oil filter, oil seal, sump gasket, sump drain plug washer	An engine leaking enough to show high oil consumption will be very messy. Clean the engine. If oil is sprayed about try to identify where the oil is coming from. If it is identified as coming from the oil filter seal, the rocker cover gasket or sump drain plug, these are easily rectifiable. Simply replace the suspect gaskets. If the leaks are from any of the other sources it would be advisable to consult your local Chrysler UK garage.
Worn or broken piston rings or worn cylinder bores resulting in oil being burnt by the engine	This fault is nearly always indicated by blue smoke from the exhaust system and a black, sooty exhaust pipe. You must consult your local garage as soon as this becomes apparent or further damage may result. You will have to fit new rings and pistons, or depending on the degree of wear found on dismantling the engine, a reconditioned unit.
Worn valve guides and/or defective valve stem seals	This is shown by blue smoke from the exhaust after a period of idling. Again, consult your garage or the Owners Workshop Manual.

Symptom Excessive mechanical noise from engine

Possible Fault	Check and Remedy
Incorrect valve to rocker arm clearances (tappets)	The noise associated with this fault is normally a tapping noise, whether on or off load, coming from the area of the rocker cover and is caused by one or more of the clearances being too great. To eliminate this noisiness, adjust the valve to rocker arm clearances as described in the service schedule.
Worn big end or main bearings	If the big end bearings are badly worn this will be noticeable by a heavy clonking from the engine once it has warmed up and will be particularly noticeable at speed or at idle. It may also be accompanied by lack of oil pressure, causing the oil warning light to stay on when idling. A worn main bearing will also cause loss of oil pressure in the same way, but rather than a clonking noise you will feel a heavy thumping from the engine at speed.
Low oil pressure	Check warning light, pressure gauge, dipstick. See next section.
Timing chain rattle	This is indicated by a metallic rattle and tinkling from the front of the engine and means that either the timing chain is worn badly or the tensioner is not functioning correctly.

General Engine Faults

Symptom Low oil pressure

Possible Fault	Check and Remedy
Low oil level	This will show as flashing of the warning light or surging of the gauge on corners or hard acceleration or braking. Top up at once.
No oil. Failure of the system	This would bring the warning light on permanently and on cars with gauges these will show no pressure. Stop the engine at once, freewheeling to park off the road. If the dipstick shows no oil in the sump search for the reason for the loss. If the sump is full, send for a garage.
False warning	Warning lights do sometimes cry 'wolf' when all is in order. If no gauge is fitted get a garage to bring a new warning light sender to the car. Do not drive the car till the defect is located. On cars with gauges a complete failure of the instrument is most unlikely. Rather will its behaviour become erratic, or its complete failure will be accompanied by an oil leak. Genuine complete loss of oil pressure will usually be accompanied by bearing clatter from the engine.
Worn engine	When hot the gauge may read low, or the warning light flash, particularly at idle. Drive gently and consult your garage.

Electrical Failures

Symptom One or some lights do not come on when switch is operated

Possible Fault	Check and Remedy
Defective bulb(s)	Replace the bulb in question. To make sure that it really is the bulb that is at fault check it in another location known to be functioning correctly.
Blown fuse	Replace the fuse. If it blows again, consult an electrician.
Dirty or corroded connections at bulb holder	If the suspect bulb works in another holder then its own holder must be at fault. Thoroughly clean up the connector and bulb holder itself.

Symptom No lights come on at all when switch is operated but other electrical components work

Possible Fault	Check and Remedy
Faulty light switch or broken wire	Electrical faults of this type are very difficult to trace, particularly at night. Check that all visible leads to the head and tail lights and switch are intact. Be especially careful not to knock contacts when feeling for loose or hot wiring. Use the wiring diagram to help you identify the relevant wires but if you are in any doubt do not touch them as you may make final diagnosis and remedy more difficult. Call in a garage which should be able to fix at least a temporary repair. It is dangerous to proceed at night, even if very slowly, without lights.

Symptom When engine is running ignition warning light fails to go out

Possible Fault	Check and Remedy
Loose or broken fan belt	Tighten or renew the fan belt as necessary.
Dynamo/Alternator not functioning correctly	Check that the leads from the control box to the dynamo/alternator are firmly attached and that one has not come loose from its terminal.
Control box not functioning correctly	The operating of the control box or dynamo/alternator will have to be checked and this should be entrusted to your local garage or car electrical specialist.

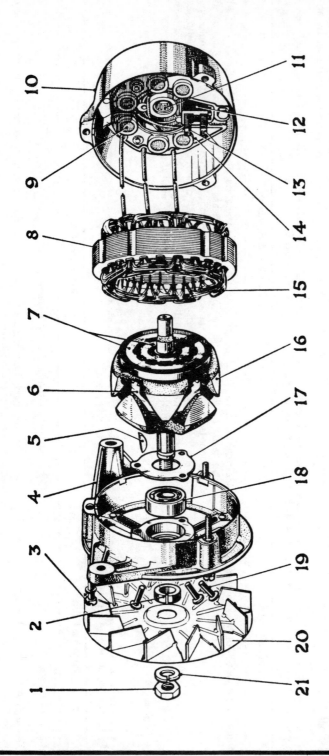

Alternator — exploded view

1 Shaft nut
2 Bearing collar
3 'Through' fixing bolts (3)
4 Drive end bracket
5 Woodruff key
6 Rotor (field) winding
7 Slip rings

8 Stator laminations
9 Silicon diodes
10 Slip-ring end cover
11 Needle roller bearing
12 Brush box moulding
13 Brushes
14 Diode heat sink

15 Stator windings
16 Rotor
17 Bearing retaining plate
18 Ball bearing
19 Bearing retaining plate rivets
20 Cooling fan
21 Spring washer

Electrical Failures

Symptom Battery goes flat very quickly yet ignition warning light goes out normally

Possible Fault	Check and Remedy
Battery defective	Check the specific gravity of the electrolyte in the battery. If one cell appears to be lower than the others then the battery may be defective and not holding its charge.
Fan belt loose and slipping	Tighten fan belt.
Dynamo/Alternator output not enough to charge	Check dynamo/alternator output as detailed above, if output low check brushes as shown in the 10,000 service schedule. If these are satisfactory have the dynamo checked over by an expert in conjunction with the control box.
Control box not operating correctly	Have an expert check the operation of the control box in conjunction with the dynamo/alternator.
Constant electric drain	Try taking off a battery terminal when the car is left idle. If this gives a cure get an electrician to trace the fault.

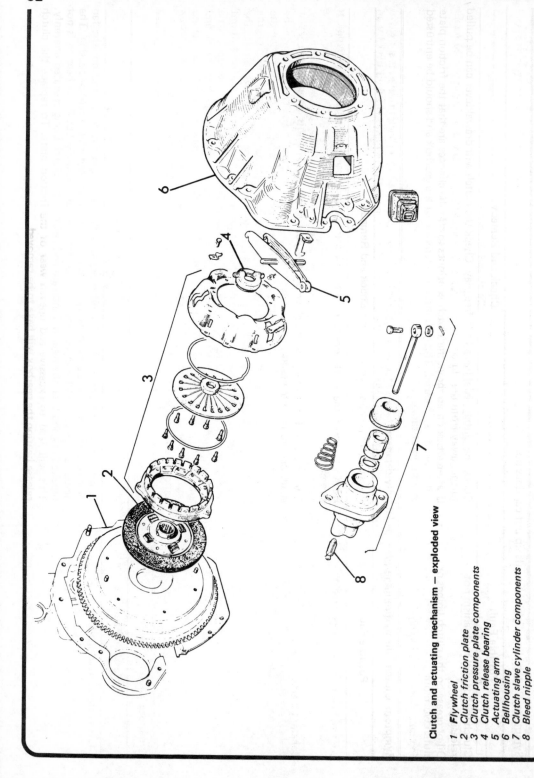

Clutch and actuating mechanism — exploded view

1 Flywheel
2 Clutch friction plate
3 Clutch pressure plate components
4 Clutch release bearing
5 Actuating arm
6 Bellhousing
7 Clutch slave cylinder components
8 Bleed nipple

Clutch Defects

Symptom Clutch slips: Engine speeds up but car does not

Possible Fault	Check and Remedy
Clutch withdrawal mechanism not releasing	Check the clutch pedal has a little free play. Check the clutch withdrawal lever can be pulled further away from the clutch.
Oil or grease on the clutch linings or clutch worn out	If after checking as above the clutch continues to slip the chances are that the friction plate will have to be renewed. This will mean the removal of the gearbox and should be entrusted to your local garage.

Symptom Clutch fails to disengage when pedal fully depressed

Possible Fault	Check and Remedy
Loss of hydraulic fluid or air in the system	If moving, push the gear lever into the neutral position and coast to a safe stopping point. If stationary, do not jam the car into gear. Remain parked and inspect. Check to see if the clutch release lever operates when an assistant presses the pedal. If the fluid has leaked away, refilling the reservoir may give a temporary cure, but leaking fluid will ruin paint.
Clutch disc sticking to pressure plate or release bearing very badly worn	If the hydraulic system is found to be operating satisfactorily one of these two faults may be apparent. These faults will almost invariably be associated with squeals and noises when the clutch pedal is operated. Check by stopping the engine, engaging a gear, depressing the clutch and putting on the handbrake. Then try to start the engine. If it refuses to turn, the clutch is stuck solid amd must be removed and examined. If the engine is started without difficulty try using the clutch in the normal manner. If the drive continues to 'creep' a little when the pedal is fully depressed, carry on slipping the clutch for a few moments to try and rub off whatever may have been on the friction surfaces as a temporary measure. If no improvement of any kind results there must be a serious defect which will require gearbox removal and examination of the clutch. This again is not an instant repair.

Symptom Clutch squeal

Possible Fault	Check and Remedy
Clutch release bearing worn	Squealing noises from the clutch (and make sure they are from the clutch and not the fan belt or water pump) are most likely to come from a worn out clutch release bearing. The actual efficiency of the clutch may not be affected immediately but if the bearing is not repaired in good time the wear will increase and result in the clutch being operated unevenly. This will lead to excessive and uneven wear of the friction plate. To replace the clutch release bearing the gearbox will have to be removed.

Brake Defects

Symptom Pedal feels spongy when the brakes are applied

Possible Fault	Check and Remedy
Air present in the hydraulic system	Bleed the hydraulic system as described earlier and check for leaks where air could have entered the system.

Symptom Stopping ability poor though pedal pressure is hard

Possible Fault	Check and Remedy
Brake pads or linings excessively worn	Examine and renew as necessary.
Brake pads or linings contaminated with oil or hydraulic fluid	Examine the brake pads and linings if found to be contaminated renew them. Also look for the source of contamination and eliminate it if possible, otherwise consult your local garage for advice.
One or more of the wheel cylinders seized	Remove the brake pads one at a time as detailed in the 5000 mile service schedule. Look at the disc surface. It should be bright and shiny. If rusty, the brake cylinder is seized. If a seized cylinder is located consult your local garage for a replacement to be fitted. If the rear brakes are suspect, investigation and replacement are best left to your local Chrysler UK agent.

Symptom Car pulls to one side when brakes are applied

Possible Fault	Check and Remedy
Brake pads or linings on one side (opposite side from pull) are contaminated with oil or hydraulic fluid	Examine the pads and linings. Renew them as necessary.
Unequal wear on brake pads or linings	Check the wheel cylinders as described above and have them replaced as necessary.
Wheel cylinder seized (on opposite side from pull)	Check the wheel cylinders as described above and have them replaced as necessary.

Symptom Brake pedal travels right to the floor with little or no resistance and brakes are virtually useless

Possible Fault	Check and Remedy
Bad leak in hydraulic system resulting in considerable loss of fluid and no pressure being applied to wheel cylinders, or master cylinder internal seals have failed	This fault is usually rather sudden and if you are lucky enough not to have hit anything, do not under any circumstances, attempt to drive the car any further. Apart from it being very dangerous you will be contravening the law. Check the wheel cylinder hydraulic pipes and rubbers immediately for a hydraulic leak; if no leak is apparent then the master cylinder seals have failed. Call a breakdown vehicle and get the job done professionally making sure that the braking system is thoroughly tested after repair. Do not drive the car, there is no 'roadside' remedy.

Symptom Brake juddering

Possible Fault	Check and Remedy
Brake discs badly scored or warped Brake drums badly scored	Remove the front wheels and examine the discs for signs of deep scoring. Also remove the rear wheels and examine the drums for the same signs. Scoring can only have been caused by pads or linings worn down to base metal, or by some foreign body such as a small stone finding its way between the pads and disc. If there is no sign of scoring the discs may have become warped due to overheating. This is not easy to see with the naked eye and should be checked by an expert with proper equipment. Scored discs or drums should be replaced.

Running Problems

Symptom Car vibrates on smooth road, at certain speeds, and perhaps steering wheel shakes too

Possible Fault	Check and Remedy
Wheels out of balance	Get them balanced by a garage or tyre factor.
Drive line defect	Get a garage to investigate items like the propeller shaft.

Symptom Transmission judder

Possible Fault	Check and Remedy
Loose engine/gearbox mountings, worn universal joints, worn crownwheel or pinion, loose rear suspension mounting points, clutch snatching	This fault is very often associated with the clutch but not necessarily caused by any clutch defect. The fault is normally particularly noticeable when moving away from rest. Check first that the two front engine mountings are secure and the gearbox mounting also. Check the propeller shaft universal joints by trying to turn the shaft with one hand, the other holding the rear axle flange when the rear universal is being checked and the front half coupling when the front universal is being checked. Any movement between the propeller shaft and the front and the rear couplings indicate considerable wear, which could easily cause juddering. If worn, the old worn bearings and spiders will have to be replaced. If the universal joints appear to be in order check the back axle by rotating the propeller shaft. If there is a great deal of free movement before the drive takes up the fault could lie here. Another indication of a worn crownwheel and pinion is a very noticeable 'clunk' on taking up the drive. Check also that the rear axle and suspension are securely attached to each other and the car body frame. If diagnosis indicates that the judder is due to a clutch fault it will be caused by 'snatching' between the friction surfaces and may be associated with other clutch faults already covered.

Symptom Car tends to wander when driven in a straight line

Possible Fault	Check and Remedy
Tyre pressures incorrect or uneven	Check the tyre pressures and adjust them as necessary.
Broken or weak spring	Have a good look round the springs. If a spring is badly weakened this will very often be noticeable by the fact that the car will appear to be lopsided when standing on level ground.
Excessive wear in the steering linkage	To check if there is any excessive wear in the linkage, jack up the front of the car and examine all joints in the mechanism by pulling and pushing them. If there is excessive

movement it is probable that replacement parts will be necessary and this job should be entrusted to your local garage. A lot of free play on the steering wheel when the car is at rest indicates considerable wear in the linkage, very often in the steering box itself.

Car incorrectly loaded

If you are carrying any reasonable weight of passengers or luggage make sure that the load is evenly distributed round the car and not all on one side as this can effect the handling and steering quite considerably.

Front wheel bearings worn or need adjustment

Check the front wheel bearings for end float. When jacked up there should be just discernible end float in the bearings.

Symptom Steering becomes stiff after running normally

Possible Fault	Check and Remedy
Front tyre pressures too low	Inflate the tyres to the correct pressure as shown in the specifications.
Front wheels badly out of alignment	Get your local garage to check and adjust the front wheel alignment.
Front suspension pivots seized	Dismantle and examine the joints.

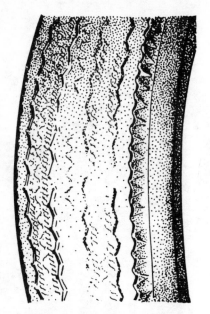

Over inflated

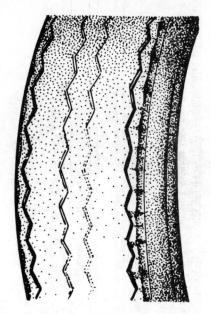

Under inflated

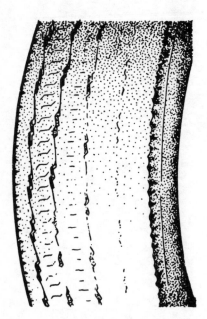

Excessive toe-in or toe-out

Three examples of very badly and irregularly worn tyres (now illegal). It is unnecessary for these types of wear to take place and, if regular checking is carried out, the causes may be rectified. If in doubt consult your local Chrysler Garage.

Tyre Wear

Symptom Tyres are 'scuffed' on the edges and wear quickly

Possible Fault	Check and Remedy
Tyres under-inflated	Inflate the tyres to the correct pressure as shown in the specifications.
Front wheels out of alignment	Have the wheels correctly aligned on proper equipment.

Symptom Tyre wearing quickly in centre of tread

Possible Fault	Check and Remedy
Tyres over-inflated	Reduce the tyre pressure to the correct level as shown in the specifications.

Metric Conversion Tables

Inches	Millimetres	Inches	Millimetres
0.001	0.0254	0.1	2.54
0.002	0.0508	0.2	5.08
0.003	0.0762	0.3	7.62
0.004	0.1016	0.4	10.16
0.005	0.1270	0.5	12.70
0.006	0.1524	0.6	15.24
0.007	0.1778	0.7	17.78
0.008	0.2032	0.8	20.32
0.009	0.2286	0.9	22.96
0.01	0.254	1.0	25.4
0.02	0.508	2.0	50.8
0.03	0.762	3.0	76.2
0.04	1.016	4.0	101.6
0.05	1.270	5.0	127.0
0.06	1.524	6.0	152.4
0.07	1.778	7.0	177.8
0.08	2.032	8.0	203.2
0.09	2.286	9.0	228.6
		10.0	254.0

Torque Wrench Settings

lb ft	Kg m	Kg m	lb ft
1	0.138	1	7.233
2	0.276	2	14.466
3	0.414	3	21.699
4	0.553	4	28.932
5	0.691	5	36.165
6	0.829	6	43.398
7	0.967	7	50.631
8	1.106	8	57.864
9	1.244	9	65.097
10	1.382	10	72.330
20	2.765	20	144.660
30	4.147	30	216.990

Metric Conversion Table

Distance

Miles	Kilometres	Kilometres	Miles
1	1.61	1	0.62
2	3.22	2	1.24
3	4.83	3	1.86
4	6.44	4	2.49
5	8.05	5	3.11
6	9.66	6	3.73
7	11.27	7	4.35
8	12.88	8	4.97
9	14.48	9	5.59
10	16.09	10	6.21
20	32.19	20	12.43
30	48.28	30	18.64
40	64.37	40	24.85
50	80.47	50	31.07
60	96.56	60	37.28
70	112.65	70	43.50
80	128.75	80	49.71
90	144.84	90	55.92
100	160.93	100	62.14

Capacities

Pints	Litres	Litres	Pints	Gallons	Litres	Litres	Gallons
1	0.57	1	1.76	1	4.55	1	0.22
2	1.14	2	3.52	2	0.09	2	0.44
3	1.70	3	5.28	3	13.64	3	0.66
4	2.27	4	7.04	4	18.18	4	0.88
5	2.84	5	8.80	5	22.73	5	1.10
6	3.41	6	10.56	6	27.28	6	1.32
7	3.98	7	12.32	7	31.82	7	1.54
8	4.55	8	14.08	8	36.37	8	1.76
9	5.11	9	15.841	9	40.91	9	1.98
10	5.58	10	17.60	10	45.46	10	2.20
11	6.25	11	19.36	11	50.01	20	4.40
12	6.82	12	21.12	12	54.56	30	6.60

Metric Conversion Table

Tyre Pressures

lb/sq in	Kg/sq cm	Kg/sq cm	lb/sq in
1	0.07	1	14.22
2	0.14	2	28.50
3	0.21	3	42.67
4	0.28	4	56.89
5	0.35	5	71.12
6	0.42	6	85.34
7	0.49	7	99.56
8	0.56	8	113.79
9	0.63	9	128.00
10	0.70	10	142.23
20	1.41	20	284.47
30	2.11	30	426.70

Inches	Decimals	Millimetres
1/64	0.0156	0.3969
1/32	0.0313	0.7937
1/16	0.0625	1.5875
1/8	0.125	3.1750
3/16	0.1875	4.7625
1/4	0.25	6.3500
5/16	0.3125	7.9375
3/8	0.375	9.5250
7/16	0.4375	11.1125
1/2	0.5	12.7000
9/16	0.5625	14.2875
5/8	0.625	15.8750
11/16	0.6875	17.4625
3/4	0.75	19.0500
13/16	0.8125	20.6375
7/8	0.875	22.2250
15/16	0.9375	23.8125

Castrol GRADES

Castrol Engine Oils

Castrol GTX

An ultra high performance SAE 20W/50 motor oil which exceeds the latest API MS requirements and manufacturers' specifications. Castrol GTX with liquid tungsten† generously protects engines at the extreme limits of performance, and combines both good cold starting with oil consumption control. Approved by leading car makers.

Castrol XL 20/50

Contains liquid tungsten†; well suited to the majority of conditions giving good oil consumption control in both new and old cars.

Castrolite (Multi-grade)

This is the lightest multi-grade oil of the Castrol motor oil family containing liquid tungsten†. It is best suited to ensure easy winter starting and for those car models whose manufacturers specify lighter weight oils.

Castrol Grand Prix

An SAE 50 engine oil for use where a heavy, full-bodied lubricant is required.

Castrol Two-Stroke-Four

A premium SAE 30 motor oil possessing good detergency characteristics and corrosion inhibitors, coupled with low ash forming tendency and excellent anti-scuff properties. It is suitable for all two-stroke motor-cycles, and for two-stroke and small four-stroke horticultural machines.

Castrol CR (Multi-grade)

A high quality engine oil of the SAE-20W/30 multi-grade type, suited to mixed fleet operations.

Castrol CRI 10, 20, 30

Primarily for diesel engines, a range of heavily fortified oils, covering the requirements of DEF 2101-D and Supplement 1 specifications.

Castrol CRB 20, 30

Primarily for diesel engines, heavily fortified, fully detergent oils, covering the requirements of MIL-L-2104B.

Castrol R 40

Primarily designed and developed for highly stressed racing engines. Castrol 'R' should not be mixed with any other oil nor with any grade of Castrol.
†*Liquid Tungsten is an oil soluble long chain tertiary alkyl primary amine tungstate covered by British Patent No. 882,295.*

Castrol Gear Oils

Castrol Hypoy (90 EP)

A light-bodied powerful extreme pressure gear oil for use in hypoid rear axles and in some gearboxes.

Castrol Gear Oils (continued)

Castrol Hypoy Light (80 EP)

A very light-bodied powerful extreme pressure gear oil for use in hypoid rear axles in cold climates and in some gearboxes.

Castrol Hypoy B (90 EP)

A light-bodied powerful extreme pressure gear oil that complies with the requirements of the MIL-L-2105B specification, for use in certain gearboxes and rear axles.

Castrol Hi-Press (140 EP)

A heavy-bodied extreme pressure gear oil for use in spiral bevel rear axles and some gearboxes.

Castrol ST (90)

A light-bodied gear oil with fortifying additives

Castrol D (140)

A heavy full-bodied gear oil with fortifying additives.

Castrol Thio-Hypoy FD (90 EP)

A light-bodied powerful extreme pressure gear oil. This is a special oil for running-in certain hypoid gears.

Automatic Transmission Fluids

Castrol TQF
(Automatic Transmission Fluid)

Approved for use in all Borg-Warner Automatic Transmission Units. Castrol TQF also meets Ford specification M2C 33F.

Castrol TQ Dexron®
(Automatic Transmission Fluid)

Complies with the requirements of Dexron® Automatic Transmission Fluids as laid down by General Motors Corporation.

Castrol Greases

Castrol LM

A multi-purpose high melting point lithium based grease approved for most automotive applications including chassis and wheel bearing lubrication.

Castrol MS3

A high melting point lithium based grease containing molybdenum disulphide.

Castrol BNS

A high melting point grease for use where recommended by certain manufacturers in front wheel bearings when disc brakes are fitted.

Castrol Greases (continued)

Castrol CL

A semi-fluid calcium based grease, which is both waterproof and adhesive, intended for chassis lubrication.

Castrol Medium

A medium consistency calcium based grease.

Castrol Heavy

A heavy consistency calcium based grease.

Castrol PH

A white grease for plunger housings and other moving parts on brake mechanisms. *It must NOT be allowed to come into contact with brake fluid when applied to the moving parts of hydraulic brakes.*

Castrol Graphited Grease

A graphited grease for the lubrication of transmission chains.

Castrol Under-Water Grease

A grease for the under-water gears of outboard motors.

Anti-Freeze

Castrol Anti-Freeze

Contains anti-corrosion additives with ethylene glycol. Recommended for the cooling systems of all petrol and diesel engines.

Speciality Products

Castrol Girling Damper Oil Thin

The oil for Girling piston type hydraulic dampers.

Castrol Shockol

A light viscosity oil for use in some piston type shock absorbers and in some hydraulic systems employing synthetic rubber seals. It must not be used in braking systems.

Castrol Penetrating Oil

A leaf spring lubricant possessing a high degree of penetration and providing protection against rust.

Castrol Solvent Flushing Oil

A light-bodied solvent oil, designed for flushing engines, rear axles, gearboxes and gearcasings.

Castrollo

An upper cylinder lubricant for use in the proportion of 1 fluid ounce to two gallons of fuel.

Everyman Oil

A light-bodied machine oil containing anti-corrosion additives for both general use and cycle lubrication.

Index

Titles in the Haynes Owners Handbook/Maintenance Manuals Series

Ford Anglia 105E/123E (045)
Ford Capri 1300/1600 (063)
Ford Corsair 1500 (065)
Ford Corsair V4 (100)
Ford Cortina Mk 1 (046)
Ford Cortina Mk 2 (056)
Ford Cortina Mk 3 (099)
Ford Escort (057)
Ford Transit (144)
Ford Zephyr Mk IV (103)
Austin A35 and A40 (101)
Austin Maxi (075)
BLMC 1100/1300 (042)
BLMC Mini (041)
BLMC 1800 (105)
Morris Marina (066)

Morris Minor 1000 (058)
Hillman Avenger (062)
Hillman Imp (044)
Hillman Hunter/Minx (145)
Triumph Herald (060)
Triumph 1300/1500 (077)
Triumph 2000, 2.5 PI (102)
Vauxhall Viva HA (059)
Vauxhall Viva HB (043)
Vauxhall Viva HC (064)
Vauxhall Victor FB (061)
Vauxhall Victor 101 (FC) (149)
Vauxhall Victor FD (076)
Vauxhall Victor FE (104)
VW Beetle (106)

More titles are in preparation

A full range of Owner's Workshop Manuals also is available from the publishers

Retail price 75p each